THE
UNIVERSE
SPEAKS

Are you listening?

THE
UNIVERSE
SPEAKS

Are you listening?

111 High-Vibrational Oracle Messages on
Love, Healing, and **Existence** to
Unlock Your **Inner Light**

CASSADY CAYNE

HAY HOUSE

Carlsbad, California • New York City
London • Sydney • New Delhi

Published in the United Kingdom by:
Hay House UK Ltd, The Sixth Floor, Watson House
54 Baker Street, London W1U 7BU
Tel: +44 (0)20 3927 7290; Fax: +44 (0)20 3927 7291; www.hayhouse.co.uk

Published in the United States of America by:
Hay House Inc., PO Box 5100, Carlsbad, CA 92018-5100
Tel: (1) 760 431 7695 or (800) 654 5126; Fax: (1) 760 431 6948 or (800) 650 5115
www.hayhouse.com

Published in Australia by:
Hay House Australia Pty Ltd, 18/36 Ralph St, Alexandria NSW 2015
Tel: (61) 2 9669 4299; Fax: (61) 2 9669 4144; www.hayhouse.com.au

Published in India by:
Hay House Publishers India, Muskaan Complex, Plot No.3, B-2,
Vasant Kunj, New Delhi 110 070
Tel: (91) 11 4176 1620; Fax: (91) 11 4176 1630; www.hayhouse.co.in

Text © Cassady Cayne 2020

The moral rights of the author have been asserted.

A catalogue record for this book is available from the British Library.

Tradepaper ISBN: 978-1-78817-375-9
E-book ISBN: 978-1-78817-387-2

Printed and bound by CPI Group (UK) Ltd, Croydon CR0 4YY

*D*id you ever feel like you could use some guidance through the jungle of life? Answers of insight to problems you may be experiencing? A helping hand to lift your spirits and show you love and care?

What if you could have that guidance and love with you wherever you go? A faithful friend who understands you and what you're going through—no matter what?

Finally, here is that companion—a book full of invaluable, uplifting guidance from the Universe. Part channeled love notes, part oracle—a collection of high-vibrational messages about love, relationships, and existence that will inspire and help you on your path. A book to speak directly to your heart.

Introduction

*B*efore you get on to the book, I thought you might like to know a little about my journey and how I ended up here, writing to you today…

Although I'm considered an expert in my field these days, with a readership of over a million, I'm a pretty "regular" person to the outside eye. If you saw me walking down the street or in a café in sunny Southern California, where I live, you probably wouldn't think I was different from any other 30-something girl there. You most likely wouldn't be able to tell from looking at me that I'm a so-called spiritual thought leader, a channeler of guidance. You'd probably never guess that I'm contacted every day by people seeking my help with their life's journey.

In fact, if you'd told me just five years ago that I'd be writing this book today, I'd have been shocked, in disbelief. You see, I'm not the kind of person you'd think would *ever* end up here. I wasn't born particularly unique, or spiritually attuned in any way. I was woken up to the spiritual connection as an adult, and it brought me halfway across the world. It's not something that I, or anyone around me, expected. So, to help you understand my perspective, let me take you back to the beginning. My human beginnings.

Small-Town Upbringing

I was born and grew up in a small town surrounded by mountains in Northern Europe, where it was always dark and raining: metaphorically and literally. The kind of place where most people are born and die in the same hospital. A very typical small-town community, critical of anything new or different.

Among my relatives, the ruling belief was that life was hard and romance was a lie... Spirituality was a foreign subject. Family was everything, and everyone was expected to conform to those values. My parents weren't terrible people, but they weren't in love by the time I came along, and my father had never wanted a family. He'd grown up in a children's home and carried deep emotional scars and resentment as a result of his childhood.

Because of this trauma, he was unable to show me the love or support I needed, or be there as a father figure. My mother thought she could compensate for the lack of love and affection he showed me by babying me, but I'm sure you can imagine the imbalance and confusion this created. There were constant arguments and conflicts between my parents—their marriage seemed destined for divorce, yet they stayed together, year after year.

In its own way, my journey through early life was difficult. However, as you'll soon learn, it also contained the grains of what would become my gifts. The challenges I experienced were also later to become a key part of my coaching work—understanding how so many of us have problems with relationships and love, based in childhood. In my case, as a teen I also developed health issues that were diagnosed as "psychosomatic" as a result of my early life experiences.

As an adult I've learned that my own experience is an example of how generational trauma is passed on—when dysfunctional bonds and rejection become "normalized" in the household and repression is favored over resolution. My father's own childhood was full of rejection and a lack of love, and so he passed that pattern on to me and it affected everyone around him. Although I didn't fully realize it as a child—I didn't know any different—there was a severely toxic atmosphere in the household.

Because I didn't know any different at the time, I went on with my teenage years and early adult life thinking that my home situation and my family's modes of interaction were normal… As

I got older, my life seemed to be going well, to the outside eye. I graduated from high school with As and then went to study in the UK. Despite struggling with health problems, I pushed myself to complete my studies as one of the top 5 percent in my year and became the first person in my extended family to be awarded an academic degree.

After graduating, I landed a fairly prestigious job in the media. From the outside it looked impressive, but it involved long hours and didn't pay much. Life in the big city was also tough, and daily commuting proved draining to my health, so after a few years I returned to my hometown. Things seemed to be looking up—until the media house I worked for began making cuts in staff…

Dark Night of the Soul

Not so long ago, I was struggling to find meaning in life. I'd just lost my job and had been denied government support for my chronic health problem, which I'd thought was my last lifeline. I was forced to leave my apartment and move into my parents' attic. I'm sure you can imagine how small I felt, sitting there in the evenings for months on end. It seemed as if there was nothing for me in life, and I felt completely lost.

There was a deeper underlying feeling I couldn't escape: In this big Universe, what could I ever do that would make any real difference? In the grand scheme of things, how was there any point to my existence?

I couldn't see anything but darkness ahead… And it wasn't just because daylight was reduced to two or three hours in winter in the gloom of the town. My depression went on for months. Looking back, I realize I was experiencing what's known as a dark night of the soul, which often precedes a spiritual awakening. At the time, though, I couldn't see how things would ever get better.

But then, one seemingly ordinary but fateful night as I slept, everything changed. In a lucid dream, I experienced a spiritual awakening where I was embraced by light and my heart was activated—with unconditional love. I can barely describe to you the feeling: It was as if my heart had been set on fire with pink love glowing as big as the Universe. It was as if the sun was shining from inside me, bursting my chest open with love… Above all, it felt like everything was OK and nothing would ever hurt again. I felt truly loved for the first time in my life.

I woke up wanting only to experience more of that amazing feeling and that golden, glorious light. It was the most incredible experience I'd ever had. I would never in a million years have expected it, but this became a complete changing point, and I gradually came to realize I was awakening to my life's purpose.

I can't say that everything magically changed overnight. For a while I was just stunned. What could I do? It was "just" a dream, after all. I had no way of unraveling whatever mystery lay behind it. My first attempt to pull the Ariadne's thread of the situation was to look into dream interpretation and the nature of the unconscious. But it really felt like there was something bigger at work. Something highly significant operating behind the scenes. Something trying to reach through. Or "someone."

Over the next few months I began seeing 11:11 everywhere I went, and I gradually started to realize that something extremely unusual was going on. My dreams also seemed much more vivid than before and full of symbolic communication. Soon, snippets of messages, songs, and visions began showing up in my mind just before I fell sleep at night, and I wrote them down on my phone, bleary-eyed in the dark over the blue-light screen...

I couldn't find much online on any of these subjects, but via a discussion forum I happened upon a spiritual healer with a satisfaction guarantee (!) and booked an appointment. At the very least, I figured, it might help with my health issues. Through that avenue I began exploring energy modalities and experienced more and more of a connection to what you might call a sentient Universe or "higher realms." To begin with, I was highly skeptical of the incoming messages, and the idea of chakras, auras, higher dimensions, spirit guides, and so on.

I'd considered myself logical, grounded in what science could explain about the Universe and our existence. A child of the Enlightenment, empiricism.

In my old job as a journalist, I'd meticulously sourced facts and referenced reality. However, as I began to feel better after the chakra work and healing, and experienced how the new energy tools I'd learned were able to open my ability to hear and feel these loving messages more and more, I began to change my mind, bit by bit.

What struck me the most, and made me keep going with this mysterious project, was that these messages I was receiving were so full of love and support. They were *nothing* like the kind of thoughts and feelings and messages I'd heard around me growing up, or had ever had in my own private mind.

My research led me through scores of books and courses— psychoanalysis; the alchemical tradition and history; the impacts of beliefs and the laws of the Universe; meditation, mindfulness, automatic writing, and spiritual communication… Gradually my experiences began to make more and more sense, and I accepted the idea that there really was something or someone seeking to communicate with me. That there was a purpose to it all.

Mentally, I was functioning as well as ever, so I knew somehow that I wasn't "going crazy." I even completed a 12-month course in history at the local university during this time. I also filed my own taxes and did a number of other things that clearly showed I was a well-adjusted individual by most definitions. The biggest change came when I learned how to clear my channel and raise my energy vibration—cleansing old negativity and programming out of my system (there was a *lot* from my childhood and family background).

I'm not going to lie—it wasn't easy. As anyone who's been in spiritual awakening will tell you, it's good but it's not easy. This whole time involved a lot of crying. A lot of confusion. Heaviness followed by intense bursts of lightness. Epiphanies. Feeling past hurts rise to the surface. But the light and the love stayed with me beneath it all. And the more I cleared through it, the better I felt.

My life gradually began improving around me too. As I learned to write down these loving, helpful messages, I was quickly encouraged by this presence of light—or I might say *pushed*, because it was way out of my comfort zone—to begin sharing them. It was shown to me that many others out there were experiencing the same kind of spiritual awakening I was going through and that it would be helpful for both them and me if I reached out. I was also shown that 11:11 is the secret code revealed to those awakening to activate the soul's presence and unleash a new chapter in their lives—just as I'd experienced.

So, despite never having written a blog before, I started a site to share my experiences and the spiritual messages I'd received, and to offer my coaching services to others—using my newfound abilities and the energy healing methods that had helped me so much. After a few months, I finally managed to get out of my parents' house and into a peaceful apartment of my own where I could focus on my recent experiences and develop my new skills. (I wasn't able to share with them what I was working on, as I felt they wouldn't understand.)

My journey blossomed rapidly as I gained my own space to focus. Via my blog I discovered that there really were thousands of others out there going through the same kind of experiences, and their response to my spiritual messages, methods, and healing sessions was overwhelming. It was and continues to be an incredible experience, and I'm so grateful to have been able to share positive messages and help with so many these last few years.

Where Do the Messages Come From?

So, how do I channel these messages and the healing sessions I create—including those featured in this book? It started off as automatic writing and I still do most of my written work through this "translation-based" method, but there are many elements involved. Traditional psychic convention would say I use a combination of clairaudience, claircognisance, clairsentience, and clairvoyance.

I "translate" onto paper what I hear, feel, perceive, or "download" from spiritual communication. I receive words, sentences, images, and sensations, and sometimes I just "know" what the whole message is about before the words come. And I put this down on paper using my human hands and mind and words.

I do hope and believe you can tell when reading this book that there's something "beyond" from which I'm sharing these messages (I'll tell you soon what that "beyond" is). What I've learned—and have been shown by this presence—is that when a message comes from the human mind it's often tainted by the ego and our own preconceptions. Fear and judgment may come into it.

When the messages are "genuine," on the other hand, you can feel it—they are filled with a sense of light and love. They are high vibrational, activating. They make you feel something deeper. I like to think of it as those messages speaking to your soul.

There's a theory that an expert is someone who has practiced his or her craft for more than 10,000 hours. Well, I'm at more than that when it comes to spiritual communication, energy and karma clearing, shadow work, healing... I say this not to brag, but to show what it takes to be a truly clear channel.

I didn't go into this field seeking fame or acclaim. If anything, I often had to be nudged and coerced along, but I don't regret it for a second. Along the way I took each step in faith and shared what had been so healing and uplifting for me personally. And that's actually something that helps me be an open and clear channel—the fact that I'm not trying to serve myself with the messages allows me to be a more neutral "translator."

So, who are these messages really from? you may ask. My old self (pre-spiritual awakening) would have called the source of these messages "the universal consciousness," just as mythologist Joseph Campbell or psychoanalyst Carl Jung might have described it. The collective presence of wisdom from all of humanity through the ages. In spiritual terms you may call it the light, source, the Universe; even angels, beings of light.

But here's the essential point: What I experienced and share in this book is that no matter what we call it, there exists a source of wisdom, a presence of love, wanting only the best for us. Through my metamorphosis I learned to tap into these insights, help, and guidance wanting to reach out, and it transformed my own life. And, given how quickly my readership has grown, I know that these messages "want" to get out there, to benefit as many as possible.

It's also important for me to stress that you don't have to be "spiritual" or belong to a particular faith to benefit from these messages. Above all they tap into the love of all beings. To the heart. And that's there in us all, whether we believe in a higher power or not. Yes, the messages in this book are from the Universe, but the amazing thing is, in many ways, *we are* that Universe. If you look up the science behind it, you'll find that we are all energy and energy never dies. We are literally made from the same substances as stars—that's not just a fanciful saying.

So, I want you to know that this isn't a book of mystical prophecies meant to keep anyone looking to an outside power for salvation. It is to kindle the light inside you, to help you see your own greatness, your own divinity. To help you remember and tap into how powerful you really are.

This book is my way of reaching out to as many people as possible with the love and light I've been fortunate to have as a guide and support on my own journey in recent years. Because the amazing thing is, I've experienced that this unconditional love and support is there for everyone! We just need to know how to tap into it. And when we do, life begins to change and expand before our very eyes. Not only have I seen this kind of transformation happen with clients time and time again, that's also what happened for me—against all odds. And I'd never want to go back to how things used to be.

My New Life In Light

Five short years after launching my blog, I'm now a thought leader in the field of spiritual love and relationships, and my writing has spread to an incredible readership of over one million people. Every day, I get messages from people sharing how their lives have been uplifted by my work. I've been able to move to sunny California, sharing love and light for a living. My life looks pretty much like a dream come true these days!

And you know what, the amazing thing is, you don't have to be "born special" to shift *your* life into a higher state with the help of this book and the messages and methods in it. I grew up in an ordinary town, to an ordinary low-income family; none of my relatives had spiritual gifts, and I wasn't somehow divinely blessed in life. That's what unlocking your inner light is all about—it's been there inside you all along, even if you never realized it.

When I now wake up in the mornings and watch the hummingbirds outside my house in the sunshine, I sometimes catch myself, stunned that I'm actually *here*. That I made it halfway across the world when no one in my family had ever moved out of the small town I grew up in. That I'm here in so much light when I grew up in darkness.

I know that if my life could change this dramatically for the better in such a short space of time, it can happen for everyone!

If I could go back to earlier in my life and give myself just some of these messages in the moments when I felt down and out and alone, I know it would have been a miracle to me.

Maybe you're at that place now and this book will kindle your light in a much-needed way. That's why this book is such a passionate project for me—I know that out there are so many people who can be uplifted by these messages. People who don't know how loved they really are, how special they are—perhaps including you. This book is meant to help you unlock your own light, to help you live your best life.

I hope and believe that it can be a lifeline and a bolt of inspiration to uplift, transform, and heal. Small and handy, it can fit among your personal belongings and be a "friend" through life's ups and downs. It can also be a great aid to opening up your connection with your own intuition and higher guidance.

I absolutely loved creating this book, and it's my deeply felt hope that it will become a valuable and inspiring part of your life too!

Cassady Cayne x

P.S. I would love to hear from you about your experiences with these messages and the essence of *The Universe Speaks— Are You Listening?*! If something resonates deeply with you, or could help someone you know in need, feel free to share it or take a picture of the message and post it on social media. Hashtag it #theuniversespeaksbook so I can repost and inspire even more people—I can't wait to hear from you!

How to Use This Book

*I*n essence, *The Universe Speaks—Are You Listening?* has been created as an "oracle" collection for you to consult when you're looking for inspiration, guidance, and help.

When you're seeking an answer or guidance, simply get out this book and hold it before you. Know in your mind and heart what you're looking for help or insight with, then open the book at the page you feel guided to. (So you can be absolutely certain which message you're being guided to, each message begins on a right-hand page.)

Alternatively, if you'd prefer to read the book from cover to cover, you'll find that it's an interactive collection of insights and exercises to assist you in uplifting into greater love in all areas of life.

Have a wonderful journey!

1

Tapping into the Feeling of Love

*L*ove isn't something outside of you. It's an energy you can tap into any time you want. The energy of love emanates from deep within you, and you can connect with it if you just begin to quiet your outer senses and mind, and feel inside. Love is there whenever you need it.

Place your right hand on your heart and say: "I love myself. I love me." Begin to feel the energy of love.

Your ego mind might protest to begin with, but the more you do this, the more you learn to tap into and cultivate the energy of love within.

I'm always here for you. Love is always here for you.

XOXO
The Universe

2

Do You Believe in Love?

*M*any people don't really believe in love. They think it's a fairy tale that people tell each other; some even think true love is a lie, a scam. But you know better, don't you? Deep down you feel that love is real. Something in you has always cried out to tell you this—in the face of cynicism, disappointment, hurt, and other people's skepticism.

Let me tell you: You were right all along.

Love is real. And when you decided to pick up this book, you were very positively acting on your soul's message to you. I want you to know that just the fact you decided to listen—and that you are showing you believe in love enough to be open to something new and to listen to your soul's messages—is huge. It's a signal to your soul and to the whole Universe that you are someone who believes in love.

And that, my friend, means love will find you. Some way, somehow. As long as you believe in love, this is a clarion call to the Universe: When you *believe*, what you *believe in* finds you. As long as you believe, you are connected to the energy of love itself. As long as you hold on to that faith, love will find you.

XOXO
The Universe

3

Releasing Negativity to Invite in Love

*L*ove is a high-vibrational energy, along with joy and peace and gratitude and many other light and expansive feelings. You can recognize these as a sense of being almost weightless, as if you're floating upward, walking on sunshine.

Contrary to these pleasant feelings, fear, shame, guilt, resentment, and anger are low vibration energies—these feel heavy, edgy, and constricted. You can recognize them as a feeling of almost shrinking, of being glued to the ground, or wanting to disappear.

To open up to and attract love, you must let go of the heavy emotions that have been weighing you down like an anchor. To experience love, let go of the heaviness. Try this: Visualize sitting inside a huge pillar of light that goes up into the core of the Universe. Every time you breathe in, breathe in love from this light. Every time you breathe out, breathe out heaviness like a dark smoke and see it disappearing into the light. Do this for five minutes and notice the difference!

XOXO
The Universe

4

Your Agreement for More Love

*L*ove is everywhere. Happiness is all around. But are you out of reach to it? Let me help you get into alignment. In order to make sure you'll be open to the opportunities and love I want to bring to you, do me a small favor. Write out the following statement on a piece of paper using a pen or pencil—or use the printed text in the book—and sign it with your name. This will help you to close the door on the past and negativity, and open up to abundance, love, and joy, once and for all.

Give me 30 days after writing up our "contract," and I guarantee that something positive will have shown up. Feel free to mark it in your calendar—you can consider it our secret bet!

XOXO
The Universe

I _____ hereby let go of any old patterns/stories/energies/ beliefs/attachments that have been holding me in lack/scarcity/ loneliness/disappointment. I let go of any beliefs/structures/ grids/energies/contracts that say it is hard or impossible to experience love and lasting joy.

I am now ready to move into my new loving, joyous, abundant, happy, exciting, blissful reality, where I effortlessly open the door to love—to romantic relationships and friendships that are both passionate and exciting yet mutually trusting and loving beyond anything I have ever experienced before.

I invite in more and bigger and deeper love than I have ever felt before. And as I share love with others, I am provided with even more love by the Universe. From now on I am always loved— generously, abundantly, joyously. And so it is.

Thank you.

Signed: _____

5

This Is Not a One Size Fits All

*I*n life and relationships, we could say you are training to be yourself and to be as open as possible to being loved for who you really are. This is not something you can get wrong! Put any thoughts of "wrongness" out of your mind right now. Please don't ever compare yourself to others, because you are meant to be your unique self!

You are learning to be yourself, perfectly, and to find and experience the love that is "perfect" for you. And now what I'd like you to focus on is learning how to do this happily. To do so, focus on whether something or someone makes you feel good or not, rather than whether it or they are "right" or not. Don't pay attention to what other people are doing but to what you feel drawn to. You were created with this inner compass to your fulfillment, and it's not like anyone else's.

What feels good and light and bright to you? That's the path to happiness… That's the path to love.

XOXO
The Universe

6

Attracting Love

When you approach love as always having to get it from *others*, you are unfortunately making things harder for yourself. You see, to seek love from other people, thinking that you need them or that you won't manage without them, tends to make the connection distorted—emotionally and energetically. It becomes about need and want, which are based in feelings of not having enough. It's out of harmony with the energy of love.

So, in order to attract lasting, joyous love from others, begin to strengthen your own love within yourself. Be good to you. Cherish you. Know that others can give you love but you are not dependent on it. Shift your thoughts. What if you were already whole inside? What if you didn't *need* love or another person?

Visualize a golden light emanating from your heart and filling your whole space. Feel this inner love comforting and completing you. This lifts you up into the realm of unconditional, naturally flowing love—and high-vibrational, mutually loving relationships. Try it! I would love to see you happier than you ever thought possible.

XOXO
The Universe

7

The Question Is...

*T*hank you for asking questions. Whenever you pray, or ask for something, or question "why," it's as if you're opening a new door for answers and new things to show up in response. Know this: For every question, there is an answer. It may not be there yet, but it is coming!

For every question asked, humanity has gone further, advanced more. Nothing is truly impossible. In the past, humans didn't know how air travel would work, or how to land on the moon, or how to cure diseases. But someone kept asking those questions and reached out. And, bit by bit, the answers came. The important thing is, someone had to reach out! *Someone* had to ask those big and small questions, to reach for the new and what people believed to be "impossible."

Whether you're asking about love and relationships, about abundance, healing, the meaning of life, about yourself or others… keep asking! I can't wait to reach out and assist. It's one of my favorite things in existence—when you ask questions, when you reach for more, when you challenge the status quo, when you invite in something new with your mind. Keep asking. I'm excited to answer you in every possible way I can!

XOXO
The Universe

8

Heart Versus Mind

*O*ftentimes, I see people so busy in their minds that they're completely oblivious to the real opportunities, love, and joys around them. People's thoughts can be deceptive, stressful, and destructive. Most human beings walk around with a zoo of wild thoughts and to-dos in their mind—a cacophony of mental activity that distracts them from joy, love, happiness...

Learn to take your thoughts with a pinch of salt. They're not all true—far from it!

In order to really learn to appreciate the good you already have around you—and to invite in more love, more joy, more things to be grateful for—quiet your mind. Even if you don't get a chance to meditate (which is unlikely, as it can take as little as five minutes a day), make sure you catch yourself when you're frazzled with thinking.

When you do catch yourself, stop for a second and breathe, relax, let go. Breathe, relax, let go. Breathe, relax, let go. Do this until you feel calmer, more at peace. This resets your whole energy alignment for the better. Now you're open to love.

Don't forget to breathe, relax, let go. Breathe, relax, let go...

XOXO
The Universe

9

Why Certain People Show Up in Your Life

*M*any human beings are frustrated with the people they encounter in life. Especially because it often feels like the same issues crop up over and over again—like a woman always meeting men who have no sense of responsibility, or who are only after "one thing"; or a man who feels as if he always meets women who are critical and demanding, or who only want him for his money.

Now, I want you to really pay attention to what I'm saying because knowing this will help you no matter where you're at right now: *You attract who you expect.* Your beliefs about other people, the opposite sex especially, are constantly sending out an energy signal to your surroundings and matching you up with more of the same. As long as you believe certain things about men, the men you meet will tend to display those very characteristics—even if they have other traits, those will be the ones drawn out in your encounters together.

So, in order to remedy this and help you attract what you *want* rather than what you *don't want*, begin to grow aware of your beliefs about other people, and when you notice negative perceptions coming up, steer yourself in a more desirable direction. Write down your list of desirable traits in the opposite sex, in your ideal partner, or even in friends. Make a list of the personality traits of your dream lover. Write down the characteristics of your ideal friend.

Deliberately train yourself to notice positive traits in other people—even if, to begin with, you're practicing with characters in TV shows or novels. When you begin to look for the good in others, you automatically begin inviting in a whole new type of person to your life. And you'll find that a new and more positive dynamic develops with existing friends and loved ones too. Enjoy!

XOXO
The Universe

10

Electromagnetic Love

*L*ove isn't just a feeling—it's an energy sent like electromagnetic waves from you into another. The Universe is full of energies, both positive and negative. When you yourself align with love, you tap into and align with all the other love in the Universe: the whole "ocean" of love. This is why being in love feels like being invincible, like a shining sun of happiness.

Similarly, when you're on the vibration of sadness you tune in to all the other sadness in the world. So please pick your energy wisely. Work to consciously shift your thoughts and emotions into a state of love, gratitude, and appreciation. When you're in love with another person, this process becomes an ever self-reinforcing and growing vortex of power connecting you both to all the love in the Universe.

Love is a natural high. And when you're on that high, nothing is impossible.

XOXO
The Universe

11

Be Like a Ballerina

*L*ife is a dance. You are constantly moving—from one place to the next, and from one project or person to the next. If you could view your life in retrospect you'd see you've been dancing this whole time already: back and forth, up and down, from side to side. Learning, growing, adjusting, experiencing...

Enjoy this dance—the more you get into the thrill and joy of it, the more the dance will begin to move to your requirements. When you dance the dance of life with joy, you are doing what you came here for. Move with life, and know that each down is followed by an up. Allow life to sweep you off your feet.

And remember that like a ballerina, you can't dance if you're holding on too tightly to the rails. Let life take you out onto the floor and help you move. Those who stand on the sidelines, too afraid to get into the dance, miss out on so much.

Get dancing!

XOXO
The Universe

12

"There You Are!"

Some souls move you more than others. Some souls are friends from before life. Some souls are ancient lovers you meet again and again on your path through existence. Some souls you are born to meet and fall in love with in a deeper way than you ever thought possible. This is one of the greatest gifts of life.

I want you to know there is always a soul-deep love out there for you, destined for you to meet. Somewhere along the line… Believe it and you tap into this. You activate it and call it in. A secret connection you share from before you ever became this person you now call self, with your current name and face and background.

Out there in life, if you haven't already met, is a love so strong it will make your heart feel like it's made of glitter or balloons. Out there is a person whose very presence will feel like completion. And one day when this person shows up, you will both feel like time and space have slipped a little out of their normal groove. Your hearts will surge like the sun shining. It will feel like the ground has shifted beneath you.

And you'll both think: *There you are! I'm not sure how, but I remember you already. I'm not sure why, but I know this will be different from anything I ever knew in life before.*

XOXO
The Universe

13

Quality Time with Number One

When you're all alone, you're often the closest to your real self—to your true inner radiance. Many human beings are afraid of or uncomfortable with being alone. But what if you think of it this way: When you're alone you're spending quality time with you!

I want to let you in on a little secret. Because human beings are made of energy, which knows no bounds, you are never truly alone anyway! First of all, I'm always around. The consciousness of the Universe never fades. And did you know that when you think strongly of another human being, you are connecting with them energetically? Being alone is just how it looks on the *outside*— really, human beings are constantly in touch with each other.

The funny thing is, the more you can be OK with the idea of being by yourself, the more relaxed your energy will be about it; and that means you're more free to attract happy relationships with other people.

When someone seeks friendships and relationships from a place of trying to avoid loneliness, those relationships become built on an energy mixed with fear. In the long run, that isn't healthy or happy for them or the other person. It tends toward dysfunction and imbalance. When you're OK with being alone, on the other hand, you attract relationships that are based in love and joy; this is because you know you don't *need* them— you *choose* them.

Spending quality time with *you* can be a great joy. Besides, if you never spend time alone it's tricky to really know yourself and your true deeper desires. Try spending some time with yourself, and notice how much more centered you feel afterward.

XOXO
The Universe

14

Your Inner Child

$\mathcal{E}$veryone on Earth is born a baby. It's how human beings "arrive" into life. Everyone on Earth experiences childhood—being small and dependent on parents and other adults for care, love, and protection. It's a system that works very well as long as the parents are balanced and happy, and have the time and energy to focus on the child and help them adjust to their new life.

Unfortunately, many parents have other responsibilities that demand a lot of them, and many have personal issues that make them unable to truly ensure their child feels loved no matter what. This means that a lot of adults on Earth are walking around with childhood wounds—of feeling unheard or unloved, or like they were never good enough, or that no one really cared about them... When someone's childhood has been less than ideal emotionally—even if it seemed "picture perfect" on the outside—it can have repercussions in adulthood. It can deeply complicate their ability to love and be loved.

Wounds of the heart don't go away just because someone grows up into an adult. So, one of the best things you can do for your love life and your health and wellbeing is engage with your inner child to help them resolve and release these wounds.

Take a few minutes to close your eyes, breathe deeply and relax. Then, in your mind's eye, see your childhood self. Embrace your little self. Pick up your little self and tell little you that you love them so much. Tell your little self that you're always there for them, no matter what. Ask them how they are and whether something is bothering them. Listen to your child self, and explain that they'll feel much better if they let go of any bad stuff—painful emotions, unpleasant experiences, hurts, worries, and so on.

See a cardboard box and get your inner child to throw the bad stuff into it. Then "explode" it all together to symbolize releasing it for good. Let your inner child know that there's nothing the two of you can't fix together and that you'll always look after them. Talking to your inner child can be deeply healing. You can uplift your whole love life by giving your little self the love, acceptance, or attention you didn't receive as a child.

XOXO
The Universe

15

Saying "No" to Say "Yes"

Sometimes, the greatest act of self-love is to say "no." To say no to what doesn't make you feel good, to what you instinctively feel is draining or not right for you. Many loving, kind people have a hard time saying "no" to others and therefore end up taking on responsibilities and invitations and friendships that drain them. Many loving people have relationships and friendships in which they give and give but don't receive much love or attention in return. Over time this imbalance depletes their personal energy and sense of self, and it creates a feeling of not having any love left to give.

Saying "no" to what you know in your heart isn't good for you is a strong signal to the Universe that you love yourself and that you value yourself enough to keep boundaries that don't allow in things and people and thoughts and responsibilities that drain you. When you say "no" to what isn't good for you or right for you, you send a strong signal to the Universe that you are worth more and that you deserve something more: what *is* good for you and makes you feel deeply loved and cared for. And these signals are always heard and answered.

When you say "no" to what you know in your heart depletes you, you close the door on draining relationships and responsibilities and open the door to what's truly beneficial to you. You begin to send out a new type of signal—attracting a new type of interaction with others. You begin to attract more love, more feelings of being cared for and appreciated.

Saying "no" can be an important act of self-love, and a powerful message to the Universe that you want and deserve more. So, if you're unhappy with a particular person, or a situation that feels like it's zapping your love and strength, go ahead and let me know. Open the door to what nurtures and values you instead.

XOXO
The Universe

16

Scaling the Heights

The human mind tends to get drawn into focusing on problems; this is because through evolution, that is what best served survival. This means that most human beings have to make an effort to stay positive because the negative bias is so deeply hardwired biologically. So in order to help your system lift into more happiness, and thereby attract positivity from others too, begin to play the following daily game with your mind. This will be fun, I promise!

Every day when you first wake up, think of 10 things you've been grateful for during the last year. They can be big or small: You can be grateful for your coffee; the hot shower you're having; the sweet-scented perfume you're putting on; the job promotion you got; a new friend, a pet, or some blessed synchronicity you experienced. Or simply for being alive and enjoying that fact!

When you focus on gratitude every day, you change your inner state and gradually also your very life. This is the kind of fun game you'll become "addicted to" in a good way, once you get going. The kind of boost that can lift your whole life's path into a higher state.

Enjoy!

XOXO
The Universe

17

The Bedrock or Flight of Love

*O*n Earth there are nearly as many different styles of loving as there are people. Sometimes you'll meet a person who's passionate and romantic and sweeps you off your feet with their charisma—romancing you with flowers and dinners, serenading you, taking you to magical places, making you feel like you're living a fairy tale.

Other times you'll meet a person who doesn't care for romance so much but is there to listen every day when you need someone to talk to; a person you know will always be there for you no matter what; someone who might not say "I love you" all the time, but who only has eyes for you and whose love and loyalty are as solid as the Earth itself.

Or you'll meet someone who's laid-back about romance and relationships but is the best friend you've ever had, and it feels like they have a missing piece of your heart you were always waiting for.

What's your style of loving? And what makes you feel most loved? Being aware of these nuances helps you attract the love you most desire—the kind of person and love that will make you feel good every day, not just for the initial honeymoon period. Stay aware. You deserve the best, but make sure you know what's best for *you*.

XOXO
The Universe

18

Let's Talk about XXX

One of the things you were most excited about when coming to Earth was getting to live in a physical body that would enable you to move, dance, sing, eat wonderful food, and experience thrills and excitement and physical love! Your body is a way for you to experience all of the physical joys that Earth has to offer—to live an adventure. Anything you can think of.

When you meet another person and fall in love, the physical expression of that love can be such a wonderful thing. But I see so many humans struggle with insecurity, guilt, and shame around their bodies. All children are born free of shame and guilt, but as they grow up they're given messages from society that the body is shameful, and that it's important (for females, especially) to keep the body covered up, to not be too open with it, and to make sure others are kept away.

I want you to know that from my perspective, your body is yours to do with as you please, and there is nothing ever "wrong" about it (as long as you don't hurt others). Your body is never bad in any way—anything your body does is natural. You and your body are perfect, wonderful expressions of nature in all its variety.

I would love for you to step out of any old beliefs and judgments others have given you, so you can enjoy your physical existence to the fullest. A loving physical relationship can be one of life's greatest joys, and a physical relationship centered on pleasure and fun can be good for you too. My point is: It's *your* body and you're ultimately free to do what you want with it.

Really, it's your Free Will. I encourage you to love your body; to love what your body can do with you and for you, and to enjoy this love with someone else too. I would never judge you for experiencing "too much" pleasure or for having been with "too many" or "too few" people. Only you know what's right for you. I urge you to go with what feels good and happy for you in life. Don't let anyone get in the way of you living *your* life the way you want to. After all, your body is *yours* and no one else's!

XOXO
The Universe

19

The Magic of Love

*A*pply love to everything you do in life, and see the miracles begin to appear. Doing something with love supercharges it energetically! Same with sending love to people, things, and situations. It draws ideal circumstances, people, events, and energies to you. Try it for 30 days and see the "magic" move through your life. And make sure you note down all the little "miracles" so you can remember them all!

XOXO
The Universe

20

Yin and Yang

In this Universe, everything is energy. You are energy. Your soul is unlimited. When you came to Earth to be born and live here, you chose to be born into a physical body that was biologically male or female. But this doesn't mean your spirit or your energy is just female or just male! Often, there's a push and pull between the energy of the body and that of the soul. Many females have more of a masculine energy expression, and many males have more of a feminine energy expression (often while still being completely heterosexual). This is a part of your soul's development.

To you as a soul, this is an exciting adventure of getting to explore different energies, types of consciousness and perspectives—to learn from many different "angles." But I see that it causes grief for many when they actually come to life. Because often, it feels like people around them don't see who they really are—they only see the surface. Sometimes people feel like society is pressuring them into being someone they're not.

One of the mysteries of love, though, is the wonder of the combination and alchemy of these different energies—the masculine and the feminine expression. I want you to know it's OK to be androgynous, or to be a man with high emotional sensitivity, or a woman with high ambition and a sense of competition. It's part of the fun of life. When you become comfortable with both your masculine and your feminine side, you will have succeeded in becoming whole inside—you will have "alchemized" yourself and will be attracting relationships from a wonderful, harmonious perspective.

When you are whole and accepting of both your masculine and feminine energy within, you begin to radiate a different magnetism—you attract others who are also whole within; others who are secure in themselves and give love from a place of overflow and joy. To balance these two unique polarities within yourself is magic to love. It makes you secure and grounded, magnetized to positivity and wholeness without as well as within.

XOXO
The Universe

21

The Roots of Jealousy

*D*id you know that jealousy is a survival pattern, something that human biology developed to keep the body safe? Let me explain. When a baby is born, it is completely dependent on its parents for love and care, food, warmth, and protection. You can see this in other species, too. In nature, the rates of survival drop proportionately to the number of offspring. When there are other offspring around, the natural resources and the parents' attention become divided, so when there is competition for love and nurturing and food, the youngsters' survival instinct of jealousy kicks in to help ensure they still get what they need.

So, in human beings, this pattern of jealousy developed as a natural "inner danger radar" to ensure survival. However, this hardwired jealousy pattern causes difficulty for so many adults. If you're someone who has patterns of jealousy, the first thing I want to say is, please don't feel bad or ashamed about it. It's a survival mechanism! Really, it means your body is doing its job excellently and that your brain is very effective. As an energy signal and an emotion, however, jealousy can be troublesome—it tends to attract more drama and problems, often based in fears that aren't real.

The wonderful news is that because the root of jealousy lies in the brain, you can help yourself move out of it for good. The first thing is to know where it comes from—*survival*. So, any time you feel jealous, click into that knowing and this in itself will diffuse some of the intensity. The second thing is to play a little game with your brain. Jealousy always deals with Worst-Case Scenarios, so any time you notice jealousy, flip the fear right on its head. Try to figure out what the *opposite* of your fearful scenario would be. In other words, what's the Best-Case Scenario?

Every time you play this little game, you train your brain to become more balanced. To help you be happier. When you teach jealousy to take a back seat, your love life and emotions will become so much more harmonious and pleasant.

XOXO
The Universe

22

The Never-Ending Flow of Love

*L*ove is a feeling, a state, a flow, a river. If you're trying to control everything, you can't be in the flow that love demands. If you're trying to push, you can't be flowing along in the river of love. If you're scrutinizing everything—looking for flaws or weaknesses—you can't be swimming in the freedom of love. Love is a flow, a state, a river. Let it carry you along with it. Stop resisting.

XOXO
The Universe

23

Boundaries

Human beings love creating hierarchies and placing rules and boundaries around things. But you know, nature and space are quite free-flowing; things move, shift, change, float, bob up and down, grow, and even blow up and disappear sometimes out in the Universe... New stars are born and die all the time.

The Universe doesn't place boundaries on things; I especially don't place boundaries on love. But human beings do. I'm not saying that boundaries are always a bad thing, but keep in mind that love is an energy—free-flowing. If I could help human beings with one thing, it would be to loosen them up a little about these rules they have in place.

Sometimes two people you'd never think "belong" together share the most special, loving bond. Sometimes two parents of the same sex can offer their child more understanding and love than two parents of opposite sexes. In times past, human beings were strongly invested in the belief that it was wrong for people of different races to love each other, and that it was wrong for couples to divorce if they were unhappy together. Those beliefs now seem outdated to large parts of humanity. Human perceptions of love continue to grow and evolve.

My truth to you is that love is an energy, and it is adaptable. Love is love no matter what situation you put it in. Your time is seeing the development of many new, untraditional relationships and family structures that reflect the truth that love is, in its essence, unlimited. Can you see that love exists and will continue to exist no matter what boundaries human beings try to place on it?

XOXO
The Universe

24

The Consciousness of Love

$\mathcal{E}$ven if you've gone your whole life feeling like there's nothing out there—that space is all dead debris and there is no consciousness, no love, in the Universe—you can change that right now if you're just willing.

Your consciousness is creative.

What you looked for, you found. What you believed and expected, you got. So you can change things. Now, if you've spent your whole life feeling that there's nothing out there and that no one is there for you, I understand that you might find the idea of a loving Universe hard to accept. However, I have a proposition for you. Give me 30 days to really show you that I love you. To demonstrate it in a way that's completely clear to you somehow. Because I have always loved you—but you may have been turned the other way. All you have to do is accept that it's possible.

Resolve inside right now that you accept my invitation. Even write me a note and put it under your pillow. Open up to the fact that the Universe might actually be conscious and loving and generous and caring. Stop resisting, and stop regarding the world and others in the same old way you got so used to.

Pull back your skepticism. Release any old hurts. Allow me to show you my love. Let go of your barriers. Let go of your old defenses. I've got your back. Now, give me a chance to show it to you.

XOXO
The Universe

25

Deservingness

$\mathcal{E}$very single person on the planet deserves love. No matter what they may have done or thought or felt. People aren't bad, but sometimes they make choices that hurt themselves and others. Once you peel back fears and negative patterns, and heal wounds, every single person on Earth is a soul of light deserving of love.

The more you look for this in others, the more you'll be uplifted into love in everything you do. People tend to act the way you expect them to, so expect the best of them and see them start shining.

XOXO
The Universe

26

Love Always Returns

If you ever feel unloved, think about all the moments of love you can be grateful for so far in life—even the pet who was so devoted to you as a child, or the love you feel for nature, music, your friends or your family.

No matter what your situation is right now, you have been loved before, and I guarantee that you will be loved again.

XOXO
The Universe

27

Love Is Easy

*D*id you ever hear people talk about how "love hurts" and that "love is hard"? The truth is, love is sweet! Love is easy! It's the easiest thing in the Universe! Love flows, it sings, it lifts up, it flies... Move along with this energy. Let go of the human stories.

Love itself never hurts. When something feels bad it's due to fear or other low vibrational energies and states of interaction. And you can heal those. Blissful love truly is possible. The belief that love and relationships are hard only attracts more of the same—above all, it's those beliefs that trip up so many people.

XOXO
The Universe

28

From Clash to Unity

$\mathcal{M}$any people experience opposition and power struggles in their relationships. I want you to know this is strongly based in the perspectives that people grow up with. I would love for human beings to stop seeing other people as opponents—it's not men *versus* women, it's men *plus* women.

Whatever your sexual orientation or gender identity, when you're in a relationship, it's not you *versus* your partner: It's you *plus* them. You are a team. You are both souls who desire to experience love and joy. But if you're not acting like a team, how can you share true love together?

Shifting your perspective from clash to unity will begin to shift your whole relationship. Try it, and see how quickly things change!

XOXO
The Universe

29

Wearing Rose-Tinted Glasses

Wear rose-tinted glasses every day! Cultivate the joy and the love! The only thing pessimism and skepticism can ever offer is the hollow victory of being "right." Being optimistic, and looking for the light and love in everything, will begin to magic your life into a new level of fulfillment. Enjoy!

XOXO
The Universe

30

Making Moves

Often, I see people holding themselves back from really going for their dreams and desires. Most of the time it's because they're not sure how other people will factor into it— what their friends and family will think, what reaction they might get.

My message to you is: If you really feel inspired to do something—whether it's asking someone out or picking up the phone after years of not being in touch, or dyeing your hair a new color, or asking someone at the coffee shop for their phone number, or applying for a job in a new city—then the inspiration, the idea in itself, is a signal that it's a guided action!

So please stop curtailing yourself... I believe in you so much. Go with your true instincts—with your positive, inspired ideas and feelings—because they are there for a reason. Remember that you are an infinite soul in a human body, and no one is going to make the move *for* you! Be brave and take action when you feel nudged to. That's a message from me that, "hint, hint," this might just be *very* good for you.

XOXO
The Universe

31

Following Your Bliss

*Y*ou don't need anyone's approval to love, so please stop looking for it and waiting for it. You choose who you love, what you love, how you love. No family, friends or other outside forces can truly change your heart. It's your job to tune in to your bliss and find what that uplifts you into—whether it's a dream job, a business, a car, a city, a guy, a girl, a family, a group of friends, a style of clothing, a type of music...

And once you've found what you love, go for it and don't let anyone deter you! Life is too short to waste on "likes" when you can have "loves."

I believe in you!

XOXO
The Universe

32

Making Time for Love

$\mathcal{M}$ any people are unhappy that they're not experiencing enough love in their lives, or complain that there's just no romance in their relationship anymore. The problem is that romance and love won't just miraculously show up when you're busy complaining about their absence—because this has you completely out of alignment.

I'd love to help. The thing is, your brain and energy work like this: What you focus on is what you get more of. You entrench what you give your energy and thoughts to. So to have love, you must focus on love and give time to love. To have romance, you must focus on romance and give time to romance.

If you're in a relationship, do what you can to bring romance and love into play again. Schedule dates, even if they are "home dates" with your own idea of a romantic setting and music; enlist added assistance from things that make you think of love and romance: films, books, songs, magazines, pictures…

anything that gets you focused on love. Make a vision board, even, including everything that makes you feel the energy of love and romance. And focus on it often.

Try it for two weeks—having your focus deliberately directed toward love and romance —and notice the change. What you focus on is what you get more of.

Enjoy!

XOXO
The Universe

33

Letting the Past Stay in the Past

If you've been hurt in the past, often the natural instinct is to nurse the old wound—to think about it; to return to the hurt and the relationship and the person in your mind and feelings over and over. The problem is, when you keep returning to the past, you energetically bring it back to life. You prevent the wound from healing.

The truth is, the past is gone—unless you yourself return to it. It doesn't exist, except in your mind and emotions, and perhaps in those of the other person. In order to move forward and be free to love again with someone else—or even with this same person but from a place of joy—you must let go of the past hurt. Otherwise you'll be holding it in your space and attracting more like it.

Disentangle yourself from pain. In order to do this, forgive yourself for the "mistakes" you made—for getting involved with that person, for letting someone hurt you. Feel yourself letting the hurt leave; you can even see light from the Universe coming down, taking it from you and transmuting it.

Next, forgive the other person. Yes, forgive them. No matter what they did. Because forgiving means you will be free again. You don't have to let them hurt you again, but if you continue to hold unforgiveness toward this person, you are only hurting yourself by keeping the negativity in your space. Forgiving the other person, even if you can only do it a little at a time, helps you so much to heal the old wound and move forward into new happiness. Try it every day for 10 days—forgiving this person. Again, do it a little at a time if you have to. Close your eyes, relax, breathe for a few minutes; then visualize them in front of you and say or intend, "I forgive you."

As time goes by, the wound will heal. As a human being your energy is always entangled with those you come into contact with; forgiveness ensures you move out of negative ties so you are free to move forward into happiness. I care so much for you, and I want you to know that the past can't hurt you anymore, unless you allow it to. Give the hurt to me, forgive, and be free.

XOXO
The Universe

34

Let's Get Physical

*H*uman beings tend to forget that they're souls of light living in physical human bodies. It can be a complicated relationship—between the soul and the body—but looking at things in this way can clarify a lot of the inner conflict that most people experience.

You see, often the body has one set of priorities while the soul and heart have another. Mostly, the body wants to feel safe above all—to stay with what's familiar. This means that human beings often feel more comfortable staying at a place or in a job where they're actually unhappy, rather than making the change. Because change would jeopardize the safety they've got used to.

Similarly, human beings often stay with a *person* who's not what their soul and heart really yearn for because it's seen as the safer option. The body might seek a mate who is ideal for procreation or protection, whereas you in your heart desire someone who makes you feel loved and understood as a person. This inner struggle can cause much frustration.

Understanding that the human body's priorities are centered around safety, procreation, and survival can help clarify these issues for you. Understanding the body's perspective—as being different from the rest of you—can help you smooth out this collaborative journey through life. When you begin to treat your body a bit like a pet— caring for it, trying to interpret its signals, understanding what it's asking for or needing, and talking to it gently to explain that everything is OK and you'll do your best to keep it safe and tend to its needs—it will relax a little more. And that helps you align more with love.

When the body is tense, it puts a dampener on love and enjoyment. You and your body are lifelong companions, so make a little effort now to help it feel safe and understood, and it'll make the journey a lot happier for you in the long run.

XOXO
The Universe

35

There's No Such Thing as "Impossible"

*N*o matter where you're at right now, things can change in the flash of a moment or overnight. Think of this: Retired couples who've been happily married for 60 years were once strangers to each other—all it took was that one initial meeting. Lifelong best friends were once completely unknown to you, and now you can't imagine life without them.

Knowing this, look at your situation with a new perspective— can you see how much can change? And how quickly? If others' dreams have already come true, there's no reason why it wouldn't happen to you!

Go out into your life knowing and expecting love to show up, because it can and it will!

XOXO
The Universe

36

The Important Purpose of Hardship

I want you to know that your path has been the way it has been for a very special reason. We carefully mapped it out together before you came here. Before you were born, we took a look at the state of the planet and chose together where and how you would fit in...or not.

If you have endured hardship, can you see that it taught you something you could use to help others in the same position? Or to have compassion when you later rose to the top? Everything you chose—your family, your hometown, the people around you—was for a reason, even if it was unpleasant or filled with hardship.

If you have had a path full of challenges it means you chose a very big and important purpose. Throughout history I've sent my strongest and brightest souls to the darkness because they so wanted to bring light in those very difficult circumstances.

You are a wise teacher in some way—an important source of wisdom.

I am so grateful you chose to come here and wanted to understand the darkness so you could bring light. I know you will help so many as a result. Please don't worry if things seem challenging right now. Ask me to show you the path to the brightness, to the happiness… I will light up each step for you.

Thank you for choosing your path, brave soul. I am so proud of you and so grateful!

XOXO
The Universe

37

Cultivating Love

The more you look for and cultivate the light and love in yourself, the more it will shine through in your appearance and in others' perceptions of you. Try it for 30 days— deliberately focus only on your positives and your good sides, and ignore any flaws you may be used to looking at.

Any time you notice yourself focusing on something you're unhappy with, shift your attention immediately onto something you *are* happy with, and focus on this until you feel your mood lifting a little. When done regularly, this can cause huge positive shifts in your life. Enjoy!

XOXO
The Universe

38

Love Is an Inside Job

You're looking outside when you should be looking inside. That's where the answers are. That's where the gold is. That's where the sunshine is. Look deep enough and you get to the core of existence. Silence your mind, relax your body, and begin to feel who you are beneath the thoughts, the chores, the words, the tasks, the names, the years...

Tune in to your infinite soul self. See it as a body of pure, radiant light inside your physical body. Be that soul. The eye of the storm. Complete peace. Complete tranquility. Complete love. There, nothing is ever wrong. There, you always have love. Function from that place and you can do, have, and be anything you set your mind to. I believe in you!

XOXO
The Universe

39

Have You Closed the Doors on Love?

*M*any people are energetically wired to be out of alignment with receiving what they're praying and asking and hoping for. This means that although I'm working to bring them what they want, they're unconsciously deflecting it. This can be due to parental beliefs they were exposed to in childhood or to their own negative experiences in life; or to societal expectations they've picked up through television, social media, and news.

Beliefs and patterns are all energy and they can make people "stuck" for receiving love and positivity. So this coming week, help me to help you open the doors to love once more. Every morning when you wake up and every night before you go to bed, use the following affirmation to start inviting in love, positivity, and your dreams coming true:

"I am an excellent receiver of love. I am openly and gratefully receiving all the amazing, joyous things and love the Universe is working to bring to me. Thank you! Thank you! Thank you!"

Really *feel* the energy of having received—knowing it's on its way. Now you're in alignment. Now the doors are open again. Now you receive.

XOXO
The Universe

40

Nurturing Love

When was the last time you did something purely for fun, purely for the love of it? When was the last time you had a real belly laugh, rolling over laughing? When was the last time you did something you love doing, just because you love it?

Laughter and amusement are extremely high-vibrational energies and states, promoting healing, stability, lightness, love, and harmony. Laughter and fun actually lift you up into the higher vibrations of love. Laughing every day helps you receive and be in alignment with love and joy. Make laughing and love a part of your daily routine somehow, and notice the positive changes!

XOXO
The Universe

97

41

Postcards from Your Future Self

What if your "Ideal Future Self" could be your guide through life? People say that time travel is impossible, but I beg to differ! And I have a fun method you can use to tap into your power of manifestation and become your own best friend! The light that leads the way.

So, how do you do this? How do you get advice, support, and insights from your Ideal Future Self? First, you visualize your ideal circumstances a few years from now... Who are you with? Where are you living? What are you doing? Reach for the pinnacle—don't try to be sensible or realistic.

And now have that Ideal Future Self write you a postcard. On it, they mention where they live, what they've been up to lately, what they're enjoying, who they're with, and how good things feel. And they give you a few words of support and advice. What was the attitude that got them there? What do they want to tell you? Send yourself these postcards from time to time in the mail. Put the address of your Ideal Future Self as "sender," even if you don't live there (yet). Address the postcard to your current home.

This method is like an energetic lifeline from your ideal future, and it powerfully helps you get to that point. Have your inner skeptic take a seat, because in energy terms this is no play pretend! When you tap into that Ideal Future Self and their circumstances, you are forming it in the invisible. Your intention makes it so. And in the potentiality of consciousness, that Ideal Future Self truly exists. Now, enlist that "Future You" to show the way there.

I can't wait to see how much fun you have with this one, especially when you begin to realize it actually works! Give it a few months, and we'll laugh together when you start to notice.

Wink wink,
The Universe

42

How to Create Lasting Love

When you're experiencing great love, enjoying life, thriving on positivity—savor it! Be in the moment! Allow yourself to feel it fully! The common human pattern is to fear what might come next; to think that what's been up must come down. This is false. A human construct. A story told.

Do not allow thoughts like that to trigger a negative spiral for you. Instead, allow yourself to float on the happiness and love without thinking of any downsides. Enjoy your happiness—be in the now moment.

Happiness really can be lasting. Love really can be eternal. Allow yourself to live in that knowledge, and feel it lifting you into a higher vibration where you're completely out of alignment with anything negative. Cultivate more happiness and lasting love by enjoying being happy and dwelling in the feelings of love whenever they're present!

Doesn't that feel so much better than worrying it might not last?

XOXO
The Universe

43

True Romance

When was the last time you did something romantic for *yourself*? Dressing in clothes that make you feel attractive, spending some time pampering yourself, taking a bubble bath, going for a leisurely stroll in the park at sunset, serenading yourself with romantic songs, or gazing at the stars...

Pampering and romancing yourself is an underestimated way of getting into the energy vibration of attracting even more romance from someone else. When you are glowing with appreciation and love for yourself, you become magnetic to love and irresistible to your desired romantic counterpart—even if you haven't met them yet. Enjoy pampering and loving yourself, and notice how you attract loving, happy interactions with others too.

Win-win!

XOXO
The Universe

44

How to Make Hurt Less Hurtful

When you feel abused or hurt or angered by someone's harmful or disrespectful behavior toward you, the natural human reaction is to go over the situation mentally and emotionally, again and again. To delve into feelings and thoughts of resentment and anger and indignation, and even to discuss the hurt with others so you can hear their sympathy with your side of events.

The problem with this is that in energy terms, you are now "owning" the hurt, making it a part of you, embedding it in your energy field; and, unfortunately, creating and attracting more of the same. When you do this, you are accepting the role of the victim, which is not an empowered or accurate role for you as a soul. It is opposed to the happiness and love you deserve and want.

So instead, try writing down the hurt on a piece of paper, as this expels the thoughts and emotions from your system. Really get every drop of your emotion and the situation onto paper until you feel there's nothing left, and then burn or tear up this paper in a safe place to symbolize that you're done with the hurt.

Now, your energy is not negatively impacted as deeply by the event. You are freer to move on into happiness, away from the situation. You don't have to let the person hurt you again, of course, but make sure you let go of the feelings and emotions around the situation as much as possible, so they don't stay stuck in your space and torment you.

Make this a habit and you'll see that you're soon able to shift out of any negative feelings much more quickly. You're now learning the ancient art of detachment—which is what true spiritual masters embody—and eventually, nothing can hurt you. The miracle then is that you will be more and more free from hurt and conflict because you won't be attracting it any longer.

XOXO
The Universe

45

Love Notes from the Beyond

I'm always talking to you—working to bring you the love and the wonders you have been hoping and asking for. Messages are coming to you all the time, in many different forms and ways. Feathers on your path or on your clothes; recurring number sequences; repeating images and animal archetypes along your way; dreams; flashes of insight and songs popping into your head; codes; cards that seem to be speaking to you...

The more you begin to notice and engage with these messages, the more insights you will get. It becomes magic to uplift your life, and you become more open to the love I'm working to bring you! So keep your eyes and ears open—which secret signs and messages have you been receiving lately?

XOXO
The Universe

46

Self-Love

*R*emember to be good to yourself. Most human beings look to others to help them feel good, taken care of and safe, not realizing that this keeps them in an energy of disempowerment and always needing and wanting outsiders—perpetuating the energy of lack and not feeling enough on their own.

Now, having said that, I want you to know this is one of the earliest patterns a human being develops. It's the first pattern in the interaction between mother and baby, so it's not an easy one to shift out of. But try this: What if you could be your own "caretaker" or your own "loving mother" or "doting father"? By being good to yourself, you can strengthen your own energy and feel whole and loved in a completely new way. Use the following affirmation to shift into a more and more positive relationship with yourself.

Say, hand on heart: "I love Myself. I love Me. I love loving Myself. I am deserving of love, and I take excellent care of myself. I am always loved."

Words are so powerful. Feel how they begin to shift your energy and emotions as you say them. Lighting up these parts of your consciousness will effortlessly begin to impact the choices you make, the way you think about yourself, the actions you take, the things and people you attract. All you need to do is shift into the energy of those words. Move into love from the inside out. Your ego may object to start with, but over time you'll feel the positive effect of these words more and more.

Use this powerful affirmation for 30 days and experience the changes: "I love Myself. I love Me. I love loving Myself. I am deserving of love, and I take excellent care of myself. I am always loved."

Enjoy!

XOXO
The Universe

47

The Wonder of You

*N*o one else is like you. In all the world, only you exist in this exact, unique way—with your exact talents and gifts, your likes and dislikes, your innate passions, and your experiences. Now, if there are over 7.5 billion people on planet Earth and no one else is like you, that must mean I've got some pretty special plans for you, wouldn't you think?

Try to stop worrying so much, and let me show you. You are such a special being in this big world—never forget that. You are so valuable, and I love you so dearly.

I wouldn't have made you any other way!

XOXO
The Universe

48

Natural Love

When a bird flies, it's in the element of love—in perfect alignment with the essence of its being. When a fish swims, it's aligned with its own perfect self, effortlessly. What's your element? When do you feel perfectly like yourself, maybe even without trying very hard? Is it when playing or running? When writing? When helping others? When painting or negotiating or cooking or singing?

Notice this, because it's your essence being revealed to you—the outer circumstances and energies blending perfectly with your inner soul's essence. The flow of creation and love opens up wide when you're in this state—this is you, being in the energy of love; being who you came here to be; being who you were all along, before anyone gave you a name or an address or a job and all the rest of it.

When you are in alignment with your deeper essence, you become magnetic to love from others. Dwell in this state often, and experience the world being more open and loving to you than you ever thought possible. Remember, you are you for a reason. Loving blessings to you!

XOXO
The Universe

49

Your Reserved Spot

There is a very particular spot reserved for you in this world and very special people and experiences lined up for you along the way. If you want to know what and who that is, let me give you a hint—it's exactly what and who you are most passionate and loving about!

Follow your passions and your loves to their peak expression, and that's your spot. That's what your desires and loves and passions and feelings are there for—a compass. To get to your ideal, simply follow your "bliss." Go with what feels good and right and light. You don't have to know the whole path right now, just take each inspired step as it shows up with those feelings of love and passion, and I'll take care of the rest.

It's a pretty ideal system, don't you think?

XOXO
The Universe

50

Inviting in Love

The more you can love yourself and honor your own unique qualities, the more you uplift yourself to receive love from others too. Every morning when you wake up, say to your mirror image, "I love you." Really get into the feeling of it.

Every morning, think of one thing you are grateful for—about yourself and your life, your qualities, traits, and skills. Repeat again last thing before bed. Practice this every day for 30 days, and you'll experience your energy and your life shifting before your very eyes.

XOXO
The Universe

51

Ho'oponopono

"I'm sorry, please forgive me, thank you, I love you."

This ancient Hawaiian prayer can heal your worries, solve your doubts, and release you from conflict and negativity. These words really have the power to shift and uplift your feelings and your energy: "I'm sorry, please forgive me, thank you, I love you."

Repeat as needed, for as long and as often as feels good. With this mantra you will notice peace and love radiating ever more in your life. It really lifts you into the high energies of love and peace.

Most importantly, don't forget to say it to yourself.

XOXO
The Universe

52

Releasing Fear and Burdens

I'm your number one fan, and I always have been. I often wish you'd stop being so hard on yourself. You don't realize how your perspective on yourself is so much stricter than everyone else's would ever be! Let me show you how good you really are.

You can afford to relax. Take three deep breaths in and out; unclench your muscles and lower your shoulders; close your eyes; open up your heart and let go of all your problems and fears. Send them up to the Universe, into the light (all you have to do is set the intention—you can even imagine my "arms" coming down to receive your burdens, if that makes it feel more real to you).

I promise that I'll handle it all for you. You do what you can to enjoy your life, and I'll do everything I can to support you along the way.

Love, always,
The Universe

53

Weeds versus Flowers

*T*here is a common human pattern that has evolved biologically through the survival of thousands of generations of ancestors—always being on the lookout for the danger, the negativity, and the problem in situations.

This instinctive first reaction is embedded deeply in the psyche and the brain of human beings, for survival reasons. Unfortunately, it keeps so many people from really feeling and appreciating the love and joy around them. This means they often get caught up in the tiny problem or negative 2 percent of something rather than seeing the positive 98 percent of it.

Remember that if you tend to be distracted by the one weed in the flowerbed rather than seeing all the beautiful flowers blooming, or if you're struck by the one negative person talking to you instead of focusing on the dozens of other positive people, it's because of this human hardwiring. So don't feel bad.

In order to shift out of this pattern and into increased happiness, first of all observe yourself noticing the negativity or the problems. Make light of it—even laugh at how silly you're being—and resolve to think differently, for your own sanity and happiness. Being aware of the pattern is the first step to moving out of it and into greater happiness and positive focus.

Next, make an effort to steer yourself into positivity by listing the things you're grateful for, or noting down the joyous aspects of your life and surroundings and deliberately focusing on these. You really can cultivate positivity. Even if there are "weeds" in the world, there will always be "flowers" too. You can spend life seeing the few weeds and flaws, or appreciate the flowers and the beauty. It's all about perspective.

XOXO
The Universe

54

Multifaceted Love

*M*ost human beings associate love with interpersonal relationships, romance, marriage, dating... But this is only one side of the story. Love is multifaceted. Don't forget yourself! Loving yourself is essential on your life's journey. Hold your hand on your heart and imagine sending love into yourself, as you would love a child or a pet—pure love. Feel the warmth of love uplifting you. Love yourself and be good to you, and experience your whole life uplifted.

XOXO
The Universe

55

Love as a Miracle

*L*ove heals, love builds bridges, love uplifts. Not just in name but in energy. Applying love to any work you do or relationships you have, will uplift them and enhance them. Sending love to someone who is sick will help them to heal. If you yourself are feeling unwell, sending love into your own body will help your body heal.

Sending love into your day when you wake up in the morning helps you attract happy experiences. Sending love to someone who is worried will help them to step out of fear.

Love really is a miracle worker. Try it, and prepare to be amazed.

XOXO
The Universe

56

Connecting with the Universe

*L*ove is the line of communication between you and the Universe, between you and your soul. Love is the frequency that opens you up to your infinite self and the greater consciousness. Move into your heart with the frequency of love, and feel yourself connected to the whole Universe. Love breaks down all barriers.

XOXO
The Universe

57

What Kind of Love Do You Desire?

When you set the intention that you would like to experience love, try to be as specific as you can, so you're accurately attracting what you truly desire. Would you like to experience passion and romance? Or do you mean companionship with someone who can be your best friend *and* your lover? Or all of the above?

Are you looking for someone who will make you weak at the knees for months of amazement and joy, or someone to be your trusted husband or wife for life? The more specific you can get, the more accurately you send out the signal and invite it in. Being accurate helps you attract what you truly desire.

Try writing down 10 traits you would like to experience in another person, and 10 things you'd like to feel or experience when you're together. If you're already with a partner, this exercise will help you focus on the positives and draw out more of this from them. You start to deliberately attract your desires.

XOXO
The Universe

58

Everything Is for a Reason

$\mathcal{E}$very relationship you've ever been in has been there for a reason. If it was hard, challenging, difficult, it was for a reason. If it was joyous and amazing but short-lived, it was for a reason. Everyone you meet is your teacher, and you are their teacher too. When you begin to embrace the lessons in life and in love, you can learn what they were telling you and move on to more joyous relationships.

As an example, did you have a string of short-lived romances with people who were completely unreliable? Or have you been with people who were emotionally unavailable? What was it inside you that could have attracted that? What was the learning gift in this experience?

Look at how your relationship with your father and other men, or your mother and other women, might have been during your childhood. If you notice repeating relationship patterns you're unhappy with, find the root of the issue (most often it's childhood!) and visualize yourself taking this old hurt out of your heart, placing it in a cardboard box and exploding it to symbolize that you're done with it for good.

Vow to be done with whatever was unhappy about the past and move on to something more positive. When you illuminate the root of the hurt, you can heal the wounds and move on.

XOXO
The Universe

59

Eternal Love

Your relationship with yourself is eternal. No matter who else comes and goes in your life, you will always be in a relationship with you. It's the template for all the other relationships in your life. If you learn to show love for yourself and embrace yourself, can you see how wonderful life could be?

XOXO
The Universe

60

Are You Letting the Universe Love You?

*B*eliefs about the Universe often mirror experiences with the father figure in early life. Those whose father is present, loving, and supportive tend to grow up with a feeling that the Universe supports them and has their best interests at heart (which I do!)

Those who grow up with absent, emotionally distant, or even punitive fathers and authority figures, on the other hand, understandably tend to develop the feeling that the Universe is removed or critical; or that I keep sending negative lessons to learn; or that they're unlucky. Or even that the Universe is completely barren of love or consciousness.

What's happened with these people is that their belief systems and energy grids have become blocked as a result of those early hurtful experiences. This means that although there is love available to them, they keep deflecting it. If these people could realize what's going on, let go and open up to love, they would understand how truly amazing life can be.

If you're one of these people, take a deep breath, resolve to leave the past behind, and visualize opening your heart to the light. See light filling your heart, and see all old hurt and negativity being whooshed up into the light never to come back. Now the lines are uncrossed. Now you're open to the truth—you are always loved.

XOXO
The Universe

61

The Essence of Who You Are

Here's a secret. You might have forgotten it along the way, but the truth is, you've always known it deep down. *You are love.* Love isn't something you *have*. It's not something you find *outside* yourself. Stop looking for love. You already have it. It's already in you. You are love.

Think about the newborn baby—arriving pure and innocent into the world and wanting only to be fed, to be loved, and to love. The desire for receiving and giving love is one of the most primal of human needs and gifts, and it wouldn't be so if you weren't born with love inside you: A heart that already had love in it; a soul who was already love in its essence.

Relax into the knowing that love is who you are, and feel your state of mind and your body shifting. Now you're open. Now you're in alignment with more and more love.

XOXO
The Universe

62

Being Your Own Protector

*E*very day, stand guard at the door of your mind—do not let in anything that doesn't serve you. Would you let an angry stranger into your house? Thoughts, images, and feelings can be just as damaging, so be sure to invite in what contributes positively to your journey, not what pulls you down.

This may seem simple, but if people realized the powerful repercussions that information, thoughts, and feelings can have on their lives, they wouldn't hesitate to do it. Information can profoundly affect your feelings, your choices, the chances you take (or stop yourself from taking), and therefore your future and your quality of life! When you guard your mind you ensure that you only invite in what serves you. You avoid being guided into negativity by fear and other people's worries.

As a human being alive in today's world, you are constantly bombarded with information of various kinds, so this is more important than ever. When you can be discerning with what you take in, you can uplift your life's experiences more than you might believe is possible. Including your love life.

To do so, ask yourself how something makes you feel—whether it's a TV show, a book, a social media meme, a conversation, or a commercial. Does it feel icky, heavy, fearful, contracting? Then let it go, don't engage. What lies down that particular road is being shown to you by what you're feeling.

Go with what feels light, effervescent, glowing, positive, bubbly, joyous, romantic, thrilling, juicy, happy, and you will notice more and more of this showing up in your life! When you learn to use your emotions as a compass, they will never steer you wrong.

XOXO
The Universe

63

The Fastest Way to Attract Your Twin Flame / Soul Mate

*R*eady? The answer is: The fastest way to attract your Twin Flame/Soul Mate/Husband/Wife/Dream Lover is to *fall in love with yourself*! Sound crazy? Let me explain…

When you begin to see your own best sides in the way that a doting wife or husband would, to accept your flaws and celebrate your amazingness in the way an ideal lover would, to focus on all your gifts and talents and beauty in the way your dream partner would, you shift your energy completely. You become magnetized to that person and that ideal love. Try it, and see how it works.

The unfortunate truth is that as long as you keep focusing on your perceived flaws and your problems, you'll only attract relationships that keep you in those feelings of not being good enough. So make an agreement with yourself to practice being your own ideal lover, and see the magic of your dream man or woman showing up in life too.

This will help you with existing relationships too. Energy works miracles. And of course, I'll be on the sidelines rooting for you the whole time.

XOXO
The Universe

64

Dreams:
Messengers of the Night

*D*id you know that the dreams you have at night are often messengers from your deeper inner self? Your soul, which is the part of you that's always in touch with the Universe, is always working to reach you via your dreams at night.

Often, people forget what they've dreamed, but if you can start to keep a journal—even just writing down a few key words about what you remember when you wake up—you'll begin to see the meaning and realize you've had an expert guide with you this whole time! And your life and relationships will begin to rise into a higher state, at an incredible speed!

Firstly, you'll be shown what issues are bothering you in your waking life and clues for how to resolve them. Perhaps you dream about your childhood home or your high-school crush— this is signaling that you are currently dealing with issues rooted in that time, repeating in your now-moment life. And it's showing you the crux of the issue so you can resolve it.

Or perhaps you dream of symbols or archetypal animals—things that may seem strange but will begin to make more and more sense as you note them down and start to decipher them. Colors, animals, and symbols are like "coded messages" from your soul to your waking self. Messages designed to help you live the happiest life you can, to resolve any recurring challenges, and to rise up. You may even notice encouragement, tips, and advice for the best path forward if you begin to pay enough attention.

To start with, set the intention right now that you are willing to receive your soul's messages. And begin to note down the few things you remember when you wake in the morning. No matter how silly it may seem. Look up the symbols online or in a dream dictionary and begin to piece together the messages. You'll be astounded to see how much wisdom was within you, trying to guide you this whole time.

Your soul's friend,
The Universe

65

Are All the "Good Ones" Really Taken?

*M*any people resign themselves to the thought that they'll never find their dream love. They accept the belief that "all the good ones are taken," or that "it's smarter to settle," or that it's unrealistic to expect to experience amazing, jaw-dropping, everlasting, fairy tale love in life.

Now, if you've bought into those beliefs, please let go of that straight away! Do you really think I'd send you here to be just OK? The likelihood of you, *exactly* you, being born is something like one in a gazillion! You are here to experience the pinnacle of love!

I have to be honest with you, though. The problem is, if you already believe that you've got to settle for less, or that you won't experience true love, you're shutting the door on that love arriving. So, to remedy this, begin to nourish your dream once more and don't let others talk you out of it. You don't actually have to tell them about your dream—just know that you and I have this project together.

Begin by writing down some key things about your dream lover, your dream relationship. Write about how they'd make you feel, how they'd act, what they'd look like, and how your life together would be. Get very specific. You might even want to get some pictures of people and situations that capture the essence of your dream. Now, focus on this often—every day, as often as you can think of it. Your focus will be calling it to you, bringing it forth. This will work even if you're already with someone. You will begin to see a different side to them.

Know that I'm there listening and watching the whole time, making my own notes about what you are after so I can bring you those things. Your job is to stay focused on what you desire, and what will make you feel so joyous that it's as if you're floating on love, up on a cloud above the world with happiness. Feel that feeling of joy and appreciation *now* and know that this person and relationship exists already. It's just a question of getting it to you. Leave that up to me. I love you too much to see you be just "OK" when I know you could live in bliss.

XOXO
The Universe

66

How Did Your Family Teach You Love?

*H*uman beings grow up with families who most often give them love when they behave well and hold it back when they do something "naughty." It is how humans learn about love—what's acceptable, how to behave, what will make them most loved, and what will cause love to be taken away from them.

This means most adults have an unconscious pattern of believing that love might be taken away from them unless they behave in particular ways. Once you realize this, you can completely shift the way you give and receive love. The truth is that the energy of love isn't dependent on anything—that's just how families interact with each other because of traditions, perceptions, and cultural preferences. I wouldn't have created you with a bad bone in you. You always deserve love.

Let go of any old family patterns for good, so you can open up to love no matter what—not "conditional love" but "unconditional love." Know and feel deep inside that you deserve love in all ways and it will show up for you more and more from the outside too. Your ever-adoring supporter,

XOXO
The Universe

67

Love No Matter What

*P*lease remember that I always love you, no matter what. No matter what you've done or said or thought or felt. Anything you regret or feel bad about has been a lesson, something to learn from, an experience—let it go so you can move on. I never hold you to anything bad, and I will never, ever, punish you.

No matter what's going on inside and around you, you can *always* have my love. Visualize a door out in space, brightly lit up with stars and with shining pink love streaming out of it and embracing you—loving warm light holding you close. If you ever feel bad, go to the door and let me love you. I'm always here for you.

XOXO
The Universe

68

Your Love Blueprint

*I*f you ever find yourself wondering why you've had certain undesirable experiences with lovers and relationships in life, look back. Way back. To your childhood. The parent–child relationship is the blueprint for all of life's relationships.

When you were smaller than a bundle, you formed your first relationships ever—with your mother and father or the parent figures that were around you at the time. Their mannerisms, dynamic, and tone with you set a very particular imprinting for how you began to interact with others. This continued as you grew older—navigating how to be a human in the world, looking to them to see what was acceptable and correct, and what wasn't.

If the adults around you were withdrawn or moody, this would have impacted your relationship imprinting. If they were dominating and controlling, this would have impacted you. If they were loving and present and generous with their attention, this would have impacted you.

What kind of partner are you drawn to, and how does that relate to those childhood experiences and bonds? A common theme for many is to be attracted to someone who reflects the traits of the parent who *didn't* give them the love they desired—the one who was the most critical or distant—in an unconscious attempt to rectify the situation and finally get that love they were longing for.

In this way adults often end up seeking that "missing love" from the past, but it means they replicate the pattern of feeling unloved—attracting the same dysfunction over and over. Healing wounds with mother and father can be the deepest and most effective way to deal with adult love-life issues.

So, what is your love blueprint?

XOXO
The Universe

69

The Character Armor

Every time a human being gets hurt, they build up defenses in response. For every time you were hurt, you built your walls a little higher, a little stronger. I'm sorry you were hurt, dear one. It wasn't the way I wanted it to be. You learned something untruthful, which was that you had to defend yourself from other people, from love and from life.

If you let me step in and help you open up again, you'll stop having to attract that same hurt, and you'll stop having to defend yourself. Please say it with me right now:

"I am done with hurt. I know Love is always within me. I tap into that Love right now. It is my birthright. Love is who I am. I safely relinquish my armor so I can open up and welcome in Love. I safely take down the defenses because I know I am Love."

Now, doesn't that feel better? I am always here for you. You will never be hurt again on my watch, if you let me help. Trust me, and things will be much better than you thought they could ever be. Loved one. I love you. Blessings always.

XOXO
The Universe

70

Getting to Know the Shadows

*A*lthough human life can seem relatively simple on the outside, there is far more going on beneath the surface than most tend to realize. The unconscious mind is often referred to as a vast storage house of memories, facts, fantasies, judgments, fears, dreams, and beliefs. Some people refer to the unconscious as a river or an ocean because it's full of feeling content—things that aren't rational or logical. It's full of both truth and falsehoods; strange connections; and beliefs based in hurt you experienced and perceptions you made before you were old enough to understand things from a logical perspective.

The unconscious is where the "shadow" traits live—the self-sabotage patterns, the strange fears, the phobias, the irrational drama, the rage, the persecution complex, the victimhood, and so on. On your journey of love, these unconscious "shadow traits" are triggered when a part of you feels threatened. When you sense that you might get hurt. On your journey of love, it is essential to recognize these parts of you—whichever particular shadows you might be housing—and to understand them a little so you can release them.

First, understand that the "shadows" are trying to protect you in the best way they can. Second, the shadows are based in misunderstandings—they don't know how strong you are and that you don't really need them to protect you from other people or from life. Third, the shadows all feel unloved. That's why they're there in the "dark"—they are missing the love that would "unlock" them into feeling safe and open.

When you shine the light of love on these shadows you reveal that the perceived danger never existed and the shadows can be free—integrated with love into your full, whole heart and soul. Shadows are the scared parts of you, but with your help they can step into the "light" again.

Set the intention right now that you are sending love to every hurt, wounded, and broken part of you, and saying: *It's OK. I'm here for you no matter what.* This intention in itself does so much to heal. When you embrace the shadows they stop fighting, sabotaging, being so afraid. And that means you open up to more love than you ever knew.

XOXO
The Universe

71

Spiritual Staycation

Sometimes it can feel like your whole being is saying: *No. I'm not doing this anymore. This isn't happening. Love isn't real. Happiness/love/my dreams are never going to happen. I refuse to keep going.*

I want you to know it's OK to feel like that. It's a sign that you've been growing already. It means you've pushed up against your own boundaries. You've hit the point where your deeper human consciousness is beginning to feel unsafe. It's refusing to budge and that in itself means you've grown so much.

But whenever you get to the point where you hit deep resistance like that, it puts a block on your ability to believe in love and feel love. So the best thing to do is let that part of you know: *Hey, I hear you. I understand that you're concerned and you want to protect us. I won't make you do anything you're uncomfortable with.*

Then rest. Relax as best you can. Spend some time focusing on yourself. Treat your physical body to some pampering. Get some fun and laughter into your life in any way you can. Meditate, but take it easy on spiritual "digging work" and the intense focus on growth.

Just... relax and float downstream for a little while. Soon enough, the frightened part of you will feel safe again to open up. Soon enough, it will have grown accustomed to your new boundaries and you can push a little more. But for now, take it easy. Let yourself go a bit. There's no rush, and the more you treat it like you have all the time in the world, the more it'll feel like that. I promise. Take a little spiritual staycation, and soon you'll be ready to move forward again.

XOXO
The Universe

72

Who Told You That True Love Was Unrealistic?

There are over 7.5 billion people on planet Earth right now. The Internet is connecting people all over the world every second, now more than ever. People travel more now than at any point in history. Whoever was silly enough to say the idea of Soul Mates or true love was unrealistic? There are more chances to find amazing, life-changing love out there than ever before!

Wink wink,
The Universe

73

Someone to Lean on

In today's modern societies human beings are becoming less and less physically and emotionally connected on a daily basis. This can feel lonely, even frightening, sometimes. I see people struggling with this—feeling empty and disillusioned. Remember, I've always got your back. Let me support you, help you, guide you, love you, keep you company. No matter what.

I can always be there for you. In order to let me do that, all you have to do is start believing in it. Begin looking for the signs of my presence in your life. Ask me for help. Allow me to be a source of support to you. I'll be there for you if you let me.

XOXO
The Universe

74

Hurt People Hurt People

If someone has hurt you, I want you to know something: They hurt you from a place of hurt inside themselves. The hurt they felt deep down was so strong it "spilled over" into their actions, hurting you too. Someone who hurts others is never happy. No one hurts someone else from a place of joy. It's an impossibility. Hurt always stems from hurt and fear.

I hope and believe this can help you understand what might have happened to you from a different perspective. I hope it can help you heal a little more. To maybe even some day send peace and forgiveness to the person who hurt you. To remember that they were hurting, too.

XOXO
The Universe

75

Goodbye to Hangers-on

*F*orgiving your lover's exes is one of the most powerful things you can do for a relationship. Thinking about them will just keep their energy and attachments around, and I'm sure you don't need or want a bunch of other people in your relationship.

So, take a few minutes, find a quiet place, and relax your mind; then close your eyes and visualize them all standing in front of you. Even if you don't know your lover's exes, just set the intention that they're represented there. Now, tell them you're sorry if you've ever sent them any negative intentions or energy, and that you hope they can forgive you. And if they've ever caused you negativity, tell them that you forgive them. Ask them to please release any emotional claims or attachments to your lover.

Now visualize your lover right next to you and see a ray of pure light coming down and enveloping them, cutting all and any negative cords that they're ready to let go of. You might even feel the palpable shift as this happens. This is severing all the energy cords to those old relationships.

Now, send a thank-you to everyone involved, a blessing for their onward journey into new love and new relationships. You and your lover are now free to be "alone together" without other people's energies and emotional attachments getting tangled up in the mix. Enjoy!

XOXO
The Universe

76

The Everyday Keys to Love

*Y*our daily little habits are a bigger part of your love life than you might realize. With every action, thought, and feeling you are choosing whether or not to align with love. Pay attention to what goes on inside your body and mind from moment to moment.

Do you berate yourself or praise yourself in your mental commentary? Are you mainly focused on your body in terms of how it's "wrong" or "flawed" or "not good enough," or are you grateful and loving for everything your body has done for you, every day of your life?

When you deliberately take charge of your perspective and choose to send love, see love, talk with love, look for love, you change the energy you're sending out to the Universe too. This is like a secret message to me saying yes, I'm ready to focus on love now—send me more things to love about myself, more experiences of love, more people to love!

You keep focusing on love, and I'll keep sending it your way!

XOXO
The Universe

77

The Truth about the Opposite Sex

When you were growing up, you—and everybody else— heard a lot of statements and judgments about the opposite sex and other people. You might not remember it from when you were 4, 7, 12 or even 23 years old, but through parents, friends, teachers, schoolmates, colleagues, TV, newspapers, and magazines you were exposed to an inordinate amount of other people's beliefs and perceptions and opinions about women and men.

Unfortunately, many of these beliefs and perceptions were completely distorted. Have you ever heard women talk about how men are "only after one thing"? Do they know all the billions of men on the planet? Or have you heard men talk about women being only after men's money, or trying to trick them into starting a family? Do they know all the billions of women on the planet?

These kinds of statements and judgments are not only distorted, they also put mental blinders on people so that when they meet someone of the opposite sex, they might not *see who they really are*. They might just see the "story" someone else told them to look for.

Do you see what I'm getting at here? You don't want to miss out on love because of someone else's judgments. When you were 4 or 12 you might not have realized any different, but now you realize that the world is a whole lot more nuanced than that. When you let go of stereotypes and preconceptions, you also open up to love in a whole new way. Good luck!

XOXO
The Universe

78

The Many Names of Love

*L*ove is love is love is love. Many people get hung up on finding a name for what they're experiencing—whether it's Soul Mates or Twin Flames or Husband and Wife or any other description.

I have some advice for you—be careful you don't get so focused on labeling what you're experiencing that you forget to enjoy the actual experience! If you're happy, if they're happy, if you're enjoying being together, it doesn't matter what you call it!

If you go around worrying about what *kind* of connection it is, you're only putting fear and complicated emotions and energy into it. Enjoy the *feeling* of love—it doesn't have to have a name other than that. Love is love is love is love.

XOXO
The Universe

79

To Marry or Not to Marry

For two mutually loving adults, getting married can be a wonderful thing. For two mutually loving adults, *not* getting married can be a wonderful thing. If you choose to get married, make sure you're doing it for *you* and not for society/parents/friends/family. After all, it'll be *your marriage*, not theirs.

XOXO
The Universe

80

The Meaning of Life

*L*ove is the goal of life, seen from a spiritual perspective. If I were to be honest with you and tell you what you're really here on Earth for, I would say "for love." Not necessarily just romantic love but to dwell in and experience the energy of love—love for living, for creating, for painting, for making music, or whatever your personal passion is; to feel love for yourself, for nature, for your family, for your friends, for existence; to act and think and create from love.

For a soul of light like yourself, it is the most exciting adventure to get to be born on Earth into physical embodiment, and to get to experience love on the tangible, physical plane. To experience love in all its many forms is one of life's greatest meanings. Explore love in all its multitude of expressions, and remember to have fun!

XOXO
The Universe

81

From Love You Were Born, to Love You Return

When someone passes away, human culture tends to say, "Ashes to ashes, dust to dust." From earth you were born, to earth you return. For your body that might be the case, but your soul goes on existing even after your body retires. The truth for you as a soul is: "From love you were born, to love you return."

When one day you pass from physical life, it will be a return to an immaculate state of love that will feel like coming home. Like being embraced by the unconditional acceptance of love once more. You are love. You come from love. You return to love. This is my truth for you in this moment. Meditate on this truth, let yourself dwell in this truth, and feel the depths of your being expanding and glowing with recognition. From love you were born, to love you return. Never fear. I am always here for you.

XOXO
The Universe

82

Letting Go of Negativity

*I*f you're ever feeling bad for some reason, know that it's because negative emotions and energy are moving through you or in you. This could be because some old wound has been triggered by a new event or another person; or it could be because you've picked up on negativity from someone else. Remember that negativity is energy—it cannot really harm you. Like a cloud in the sky, it can pass and disperse.

Whatever is causing your sadness, anger, or other negative emotional state, the fastest and smoothest way to get out of it is to resolve to let it go. You might even want to say, "This is not me. This is not me," which will set an energetic intention that this cannot stay with you anymore. Then visualize pure white light coming into your space and transmuting the negative feeling and energy—neutralizing it and replacing it with the healing energy of light.

Within a short time, the energy shift will translate into all levels of your being, allowing your emotional state to rise up into positivity again.

XOXO
The Universe

83

A Life and Love "Cheat Sheet"

When you return to the nonphysical state after your journey on Earth is over, you'll remember how powerful you truly were and why you came to Earth in the first place. Many souls come back feeling like they didn't get as much done as they would have liked. I'd like to help you out along the way so you can get as much out of your journey on the planet as possible.

Number one, love is the greatest power in the Universe—when you do something with love, you supercharge it. Love can heal emotional wounds, uplift those in sadness, and even help those who are struggling with their health. Sending love to a project, to your bank account, to your body, to your prospective boss, or to your love partner, works miracles to harmonize and uplift. Sending love is always beneficial.

Two, although you have likely been taught the opposite, you are an infinite being who can truly have, be, and do anything you want—all it takes is for you to recognize this fact and align with it, clearing out any blocks in the way. Limitations only apply to you if you believe they do. If you're in doubt, call on me to show you how limitless you truly are.

Three, life really is a game if you make it so—the minute you start playing, having fun, and taking things less seriously, life will begin mirroring this back to you. You honestly are here to have fun, to grow, to enjoy, to love. So get out there!

If you feel that you could use a push, or like circumstances are blocking you, call on me to open up the flow for you. It is my utmost pleasure to see you thrive in your life.

XOXO
The Universe

84

Lifting Up into Love

*L*ove is always available to you, no matter what. But sometimes when you're on a low energy frequency of something like fear or resentment or sadness or disappointment, you have temporarily shut the door on it. This means you can *feel* unloved and unappreciated even if it's not strictly true.

Energy is frequency, and just like with a radio, you cannot be tuned in to one channel and hear another simultaneously. Because love is on a completely different channel to fear, shame, and all the lower emotions, you have to move out of the channel of negativity in order to really feel and receive love again.

A very quick way to move yourself up to higher channels—closer and closer to love —is to focus on what you're grateful for. Write it down, and let yourself dwell in the feeling of appreciation and gratitude. Another method is to look at inspiring photos or listen to music that uplifts you. Remember that if you're ever on a "low channel," you can use deliberately positive outside stimuli to lift you back up to love.

XOXO
The Universe

85

Surfing the Wave of Love

*L*ove is a feeling, a state, an energy. It is available to you at all times because it is a flow of energy that moves through the Universe. You can always "surf the wave of love" that's at your disposal. For human beings, what most often gets in the way of love isn't circumstances and people and events, it's the human mind.

Humans are the only animals that conceptualize and analyze their own existence so much that they have the capacity to create problems that don't really exist. The human mind can, in this way, be the biggest block to love and happiness. Relaxing and silencing the mind regularly through meditation can help you avoid the common human static of over-analysis and distraction and stress that keeps so many people blocked from feeling and experiencing love.

Try calming your mind for just five minutes a day to begin with. Find a quiet, private place to sit in silence for a little while, breathing deeply and letting thoughts and worries float away. Over time, this will help you stay in a more positive frame of mind—helping you live in a state of love.

XOXO
The Universe

86

How Will Love Show Up?

When the Universe is working to bring something to you, it can happen in many different ways. Say you send out the heartfelt desire to share love and bliss with someone and to live happily… You might not be able to see clearly how that can happen from where you're at right now, but I "see" the big picture, and I know exactly which elements need to show up, and in which order, to get you to where you want to be—bringing you closer to it, and it closer to you.

Where most people trip themselves up is not believing it can happen in the first place. If you look at your life, can't see a possible connection, and think, "There's no way that stuff will ever happen to me," you're effectively shaping your energy to block it out. So your job in this is to make sure you stay open to positive things showing up.

Please let go of skepticism, doubt, disbelief, and pessimism so you give me a chance to get you up to speed. After all, what do you need doubt and disbelief for anyway? Have they ever brought you happiness or love? Be good to yourself, focus on love and joy, keep taking inspired action steps when the next part of the journey is "lit up"—and let me handle the rest.

XOXO
The Universe

87

The Nature of Love

Love doesn't just exist between people—nature can be one of humanity's greatest sources of love. Look at flowers blossoming in spring, trees bursting into color each summer, animals frolicking and playing with each other, dogs who leap joyously up at their owner whenever they come home, cats who spend a whole evening curled up on someone's lap, the music of birds singing, the deep feeling of home you get from walking out in nature, looking up at the expansive sky full of stars at night...

Love is all around you. Life truly is a miracle!

XOXO
The Universe

88

Your Divine Superpowers

There is something I really want to share with you—an amazing secret I've been waiting for you to find out. When you came into life I know you were given a rundown of, *Here's how we do things and we always have; This is right, that's wrong; This is admirable, that isn't.* Human rules and perceptions and agreed-upon beliefs and habits.

Whether in school or at home or among your peers, you were likely told that certain things about you were "bad" and needed to change to fit in with the standard approach. Whether you were "too emotional," "too creative," "not logical enough," had "learning difficulties," or sensitivities to food or your surroundings, I know that you had at least one or two things you were made to feel you had to "fix" or change.

Are you ready for the secret? What you were told were weaknesses, were actually your strengths! What the "old society" told you were problems were actually your "divine superpowers," which you and I deliberately planned out for you.

Let me explain. If you were sensitive to your surroundings or had allergies, it was our signpost for you to begin exploring healthier ways of living, and helping humanity move into a more positive and holistic lifestyle. If you were a "loner," it was so you'd have the peace of mind to explore and create beyond what anyone had thought of.

If you had learning difficulties, it was our way of creating "spiritual immunity" so you wouldn't assimilate the old belief systems and become like everyone else—you were *meant* to go further and be different! If you found it hard to fit in and didn't have many friends, our plan was to move you away from the place of your upbringing—if you had too many attachments, you wouldn't feel open to going beyond!

Look back on your early life, and even your now-moment situation. Can you see that behind what you may have believed were "weaknesses" there is actually a greater plan at work? Please know that as you open to your own unique identity you will discover more gifts and benefits than you ever thought possible. And if you need a guiding hand, ask me to show you what your divine gifts are. I would be so happy to help with this!

Remember, your old world weaknesses are your true superpowers!

XOXO
The Universe

89

The Radiance of Love

*I*nside every person there is a source of light so strong that if you tapped into it you would never feel afraid or insecure or sad again. This light is all-powerful; it is magnificent and not bound by human rules and limitations. This light can fuel you to achieve anything you want. Miracles live in this light—infinite possibility.

Feel this light inside you. See it like a body of bright light inside your physical body. Allow its warm glow to fill your entire being, spilling out over the edges and enveloping you in a protective, high-vibrational light. Know that this light is you.

Dwell in this light and you raise your energy vibration. Then, you get into an attractive state to all those things that make you feel happy, joyous, grateful, and loving. Dwell in this light to feel safe, good, and supported at all times.

XOXO
The Universe

90

Living the Miracle

*Y*ou are a living miracle! You can feel and live and breathe the love of existence, if you just open your eyes to it! Consider this: Here you are, on a tiny, revolving planet at the edge of the Universe; on an Earth that's one of a kind and completely unique in temperature and chemical balance and geography and all the things that delicately allow for the existence of "human beings," spinning at a hurtling speed around an ancient burning star you call the "sun," with a "moon" so gravitationally powerful it shifts the tides in and out on your planet...

And this is where *you* exist. One among more than 7.5 billion. The descendant of tens of thousands of generations of human beings. Do you know how mathematically unlikely all of this is? You are a miracle, life is a miracle—you just got used to it! Draw the veil from your eyes and you can live this miracle every day!

XOXO
The Universe

91

The Surprise

*L*ove comes when you least expect it. Instead of waiting around for it, be like a butterfly in the sunshine—enjoy every part of your life, knowing that love will show up. It's bound to be a surprise somehow, so let yourself be surprised, thrilled, awed. You stay in the energy of the butterfly—floating and dipping, at one with yourself and life—and love will recognize you straight away. Love comes when you least expect it.

XOXO
The Universe

92

The Key to Love

*L*ove is an "in" to the depths of existence, consciousness, creation. Did you ever wonder what it's all for? Life, death, living, dying... Those are just tiny parts of this grand event. Follow the trail of love, follow the path of bliss, and you will get deeper into the glowing jewel of the mystery.

The key? Don't listen to the rules, the conventions, the masses. Instead, listen to the tiny voice inside that feels like a glowing pink Venus angel.

The whisper of dreams—that's love. Let it guide you, care for you, adore you, uplift you. This is your key to the inner doors of existence.

XOXO
The Universe

93

The Garden of Love

*L*ove comes in as many colors and varieties and shapes as there are people. Just as zebras recognize each other's unique facial patterns and stripes among the herd, you too will recognize "your love" when it comes along.

And maybe you have already. It can be a tall or a medium-size love, a dark or a light love, a quiet or a boisterous love, but if it's your love you will feel it beneath all the outer characteristics.

Your love will feel like home. Listen and look with your heart. Your love will always announce itself. Your love will always stand out as unique among the herd.

XOXO
The Universe

94

Life Is a Stage...

*A*cting "as if" is one of the most powerful games in the Universe. It matches your energy to the reality of living it and having it now. How you've been in life so far is a role you've been playing. You just got used to it!

So how about shaking things up a bit? Think of how you would be, act, think, dress, speak, behave in your ideal life, with your ideal love, in your ideal relationship. Then... Act, think, dress, speak, behave like that *now*!

This is such a powerful intention to send out; you're practically saying to me: *Look, I'm ready for something new. I'm ready for what I'm wishing for—go ahead and bring me the rest.* And I will!

XOXO
The Universe

95

Taking Off the Blinkers

*L*ove is all around you! Once you start being open to seeing it, you'll notice it everywhere. If you're like most people, you've been walking around not realizing this because you've been too busy with all your thoughts and the to-dos of your daily life. To really open up to love, start looking for it. See if you can find it wherever you go.

Before you know it, you'll be noticing love everywhere. The girl talking excitedly on the phone to her boyfriend on the train next to you; the lovers walking hand in hand in the supermarket; the mother glowing with happiness holding her baby; the cat curling up on your friend's lap; the dog greeting you with excitement as you come home; the family out walking together in the park; the man proposing to his girlfriend in the restaurant where you're dining...

Love is everywhere. Look for it—let it show itself to you. This can transform your experience of life. Let love show itself to you and life will never be the same again. Set the intention for the next week to always be on the lookout for love.

XOXO
The Universe

96

You Are So Beautiful!

You may not see your own beauty but I sure do! Today I want to remind you, because you've likely gotten so used to yourself that you may not see the amazing things that I do! The spark of light in your eyes, your unique features and their harmony… And you know what? Other people see it too.

Begin to look for your beauty, inside and out, and I will begin to send you more and more experiences that reflect your beauty! Focus on beauty wherever you go and it will be shown more and more to you. And no, I don't mean the kind of beauty advertising will tell you about. I mean the pretty flowers growing by the side of the road, the stars in the night sky, the rainbow-colored birds in the trees, the pastel hues of the sunset…

Nature is always beautiful and so are you—the spectacular shade of blue your eyes may be, or the deep caramel color of your radiant skin, or the way your hair falls in cascading waves over your shoulders, or the way your smile lights up the room…

Every single person on this planet has beauty in them! It's just a question of how you look for it.

Comparison and the "standard version" of appearance will unfortunately blind you to your own beauty—you were deliberately made unlike anyone else. Begin watching for your own beauty and you'll see it more and more—plus, it will boost your life from the inside out, lifting your relationships into a more positive state.

List five beautiful things about yourself right now. There is always something, no matter what age or physical state you're in! Do you have smooth hands? Is your voice soothing to the ear? Do you move with grace? Are you a kind person? The more you look for beauty, the more you make it bloom! I can't wait to see you begin to explore this!

XOXO
The Universe

97

Are You Keeping Yourself Stuck?

*M*any people live with a concept of self that's completely outdated, and this can constitute a block to love. Things like which social circle they belonged to in high school, whether they were the eldest or youngest sibling, if they went bankrupt a decade ago, if they got an A in college or flunked out, if they divorced, or if they lost their job... Relating to those things keeps the same old energies and situations around.

Let me tell you something—you are more than what you've experienced, no matter what you've experienced! More than who you've been told by the world around you. You are infinite! You are a soul of light living in a human body. Please be good to yourself and resolve now to let go of any old negativity or limitation you're still relating to.

To do this, spend five minutes writing down all your "shortcomings" and your "weaknesses" and regrets and limitations on a piece of paper. Then, get a new piece of paper and write out all new, positive affirmations. Things like: "I am learning and growing more and more every day; I am capable of anything I set my mind to; I am becoming more and more aligned with my true self every day; I am attracting more and more joy and love into my life; I am always evolving; I am a unique and valuable person; I am always deserving of love…" The most positive and uplifting things…

Then, tear up the first list of the negative stuff. Burn it in a safe place or throw it in the garbage. Really know that this is a turning point—that you're letting go of all the old, limiting stuff for good now. What this does is release the past and anywhere you've kept yourself out of love, so you can move forward into a new, happier chapter. It's not about *who you have been*—it's all about *who you choose to be*. Enjoy!

XOXO
The Universe

98

You Were Born for It!

*A*ll the way back to the ancient Greeks and other wondrous societies, philosophers, artists, and thinkers have been pondering and writing about love—what it means, whether it really exists, and if so, how to experience true love. Today there is an array of books and websites on dating and romance available to you to read and explore.

My advice to you is this: In all honesty no one needs to teach you how to love or be loved—*it's who you are!* You were born with the ability to love and be loved. Tidy away the "dust bunnies" of negative perceptions and energies you've taken on in life and you will begin to realize this. In fact, trying to "figure out love" intellectually can just create a whole lot of extra stress in your life.

The simple way to do it is this: Think about a time in life when you felt the most blissfully loved and loving. Connect with that feeling and let yourself sense it in your whole body. Got it? OK, good—now use that feeling as your compass to love. When a person, situation, book, meeting, place, idea gives you an inkling of that feeling, follow it! Love lives there. In some way this thing you've happened upon relates to bringing you love. That's all you really need to know. The rest will unfold effortlessly with this approach.

Set your compass and follow it, and your innate system will do the rest. Remember, you were born to love and be loved!

XOXO
The Universe

99

The Act of Love

When you're in love, how do you feel? How do you act? How do you see the world? What's your perspective on yourself? What sort of music do you listen to? What do you wear? How do you walk, talk, act, think? Start acting and feeling like that every day, and you'll be living on cloud nine!

The truth is, your body and deeper mind don't understand the difference between "acting as if" and "reality"—when you act as if, your whole system, body, and mind will gradually begin producing the chemical and emotional reactions of being in love. Moreover, because you are matching yourself to the energy of love you will be so magnetic it will begin to show up all around you in all areas of life—if you're not with someone right now it will begin to draw love to you, and if you are in a relationship already it will draw out more romance in your interactions.

So get going!

XOXO
The Universe

100

Why Love Knows No Bounds

*L*ove is an emotion, an intention, an energy—electromagnetic signals sent from you to the one you love. Energy knows no boundaries, no distance—when you love someone, your love reaches them instantly, even if you are currently 2,000 miles apart.

Their love reaches you this same way. When you love someone, your hearts are energetically connected by this love. Nothing and no one—no distance, no person—can break this. Physical separation is an illusion. Love is infinite. Allow this insight to shift you into greater and greater love.

XOXO
The Universe

101

Are You Unconsciously Sabotaging Love?

*O*ften, I see people set intentions and visualize their ideal, only to become disappointed when things don't show up as fast as they want or in the way they had hoped. If this has happened to you, I want you to know that the reason things aren't showing up is counter-intentions. That somewhere in your deeper mind, you don't believe it's possible.

So, how do you know if you have counter-intentions? And how do you know what they are? Here's a simple method. If you were going to describe to a friend why or how you haven't had love or happiness in life, or why and how things haven't happened the way you wanted, go through that. In your mind, even. Talk about it. Explain it. You are now lighting up your limiting beliefs—all of the places where you are unconsciously sabotaging the very things you desire.

Now go ahead and clear those beliefs. You can write them down on a piece of paper and then write down a new, positive statement next to it. When you're done, tear the paper in half— keep the positives, burn the negatives.

You have now sent out the signal that you're done with this "lesson" and are ready to move on to something new and more positive. You have now begun to shift your energy to allow in more love, joy, happiness. Well done!

XOXO
The Universe

102

How to Love When You Don't Feel Like It

Sometimes people can find it hard to summon up any feelings of love. Maybe you feel tired of trying, or like there's just no love left in you to give. Let me first of all reassure you that this isn't true. You can never run out of love, although I understand it can feel like it.

To get you back in the flow, find some "low pressure" things to appreciate (a feeling closely related to love but slightly less of a "big deal" to get into). As you find more and more appreciation, you'll be able to move up into love again, and you'll fuel your feelings of love and your ability to enjoy love once more.

A key is to keep things "low pressure." Focus on your appreciation for the beauty of space and the stars, or for the marvel of nature blossoming every spring. Think about your favorite flower, some food you really enjoy, a favorite pet, or a person you enjoy being around; or listen to some music that really moves you.

Go through these and notice your mood gradually lifting—this is a clear sign that you are moving up into love again, opening up again. Whenever you feel "empty" of love, just take a little while to "fill back up" in this way.

XOXO
The Universe

103

The Opposite

Whenever you feel unloved, paradoxically the most effective thing you can do to invite in more love is to *give* love. This activates the law of return and the law of effect, which in energy terms means that you get back more of what you give out.

If you don't believe this can possibly be true, let me assure you that these laws are as accurate and effective as the law of gravity. You don't walk outside to suddenly find garden furniture floating in the air some days and other days rooted to the ground. Gravity is always active. Same with the universal laws of energy.

If you feel unloved, the most powerful thing you can do to get more love is give more love. Write a letter or an email letting someone know you care about them; pay people compliments; give some of your time or money to a charity close to your heart; let someone know you appreciate them; even take some time just to write a positive comment on someone's page or website. These will "flip" your own energy to allow more love to come in.

As you give, you receive. Try this for the next 10 days and feel the shifts. I can't wait for you to experience it firsthand!

XOXO
The Universe

104

Getting Out of "Becauses" to Let Love in

*L*ove is to love no matter what. Not because things are "perfect" or exactly the way you want them. Love is to love even if situations get challenging. Love is to love even if you're not able to be together physically with the one you care for. Love is to know that you would always want the best for your dear one, no matter what.

Love is to know that you would love the essence of the other even if they changed. Love is to feel that the connection between you and your dear one is unbreakable by outside circumstances. Love is an energy, an emotion, an intention. Nothing can destroy or end love except the one who loves.

When you can release the human stories, conflicts, and everyday concerns, true love begins to shine through more and more.

XOXO
The Universe

105

Nature's Love Therapy

*Y*ou live in a world of energy and you're constantly interacting with it on a daily basis, even if you don't realize it. You yourself are energy in perpetual motion. If you zoomed in to your body close enough, you would see tiny atoms vibrating. Nothing on Earth is really solid—it's energy, micro particles in motion!

Your energy field/mood/functioning is actually in flux— impacted by everything that goes on inside and around you. Human beings' energy can get very tense and frantic and busy, so if you're feeling low or frustrated or stressed out or angry, like you're butting your head against the proverbial wall, go into nature for a while.

The energy of plants and earth and nature is completely different from human beings' energy because plants don't have an analytical, thinking mind the way you do. Human beings are in stress mode a lot of the time, whereas plants and nature exist in the pure essence of each moment—no problems, no aims, no regrets. No stress.

So, go out into your nearest natural area (not one that's busy with people)—a forest, a park, by the ocean, by a lake, on a mountain... Let yourself just stand or sit still there for a minute and feel how tranquil it is, away from other people. Let yourself relax into the now moment. This is regeneration—you are now being nourished by nature's pureness of energy. You are now getting space to be yourself, to relax. Doing this regularly will work wonders for your body systems, your mindset, your mood, your wellbeing.

XOXO
The Universe

106

Love Is a Repeat Show

Many people approach love and relationships as if it's mostly about a one-off event—a big wedding or a celebration, a day in paradise, a "honeymoon" phase. That can be great, but it's only part of the story. Long-lasting love is an "organism" that's always changing and evolving.

I'd like you to think of love as a garden of flowers. In order to see the flowers at their most beautiful once or a few times a season, you have to be there to water and tend to the plants every day. If you were tending to a garden of flowers you wouldn't complain about it because you'd know that those times of blooming are so beautiful—you'd be excited about that every time you watered your flowers, wouldn't you? You would probably even see the blossoming flowers in your mind as you watered the still green stems and buds... That's how real it would be to you.

So, what if you approach love in the same way? You know that as long as you nourish it daily, it will blossom into marvelous paradise days, weeks, and months for glorious periods of your life. And in the in-between periods, you'll enjoy tending to it, caring for it.

Nourish love every day by talking about it positively, visualizing it in its full glory, expressing it. With every "I love you" you nourish love. With every act of generosity and enthusiasm, you nourish love.

XOXO
The Universe

107

Standing on Solid Ground

*L*ove isn't something that can ever be truly taken away from you. But it can sure feel that way! Many people are afraid of opening their hearts to love because they've been hurt in the past. They've felt rejected at their most emotionally vulnerable, when they felt like they were revealing their very soul. Or they've been abandoned when they opened up and trusted someone.

Now, I understand that these things are challenging. But here is one thing I'd like you to keep in mind: My love is a love that can never be taken away from you. The *energy* of love is never truly gone. I'm always there, no matter what. I'll always catch you, and I'll never disappear or reject you. Does that feel a bit better?

Now, what if my love—that bedrock love that always exists for you—could be like a safety net for you? What if the security of my love could help you feel like opening up a little more to other people and to the world again? Try it. If you ever feel unsure, or lonely, or unappreciated, turn to me.

Let me give you the love that others might be too deep in their own problems for. Let me be your security, the mountain you can stand on. Then, you always know you're safe to open up.

XOXO
The Universe

108

Balancing the Scales

*L*ove is strength. Love is to be strong together, happy together, joyous together, in love together. If you approach love from a place of weakness or need—trying to find someone to rescue you, or for you to be someone else's savior—it will be a skewed relationship. The love will feel distorted, dysfunctional.

Love is, in its essence, about harmony and balance. In order to feel truly loved and truly loving, you need to be with your equal, and you need to feel whole and strong within yourself. Can you have a relationship otherwise? Can you feel love without being whole within? Yes, but there will be "issues" involved. The flow, the harmony, will be disrupted.

If you approach love as someone needing to fulfill you or lift you up, you are unfortunately attracting disharmony and more weakness, more lack. This is why loving yourself first is the strongest way to attract a balanced, whole, harmonious, happy, mutually supportive relationship.

XOXO
The Universe

109

The Day Everything Changes

*T*oday is a very important day! Today is the first day of the rest of your life! The beginning of a new chapter—if you choose it. Today is the day that everything changes—if you make it so.

Remember that every day you make choices that impact the whole rest of your life. If you want to see your dreams come true, make sure you keep making the choices that will get you there, not the choices that take you further away.

When you're out driving, you know exactly where you're headed and don't drive roundabout ways or back on yourself unless you have to. On the big freeway system of life, make sure you stay in the lane that will take you to where you want to go, not in the turn-offs that move you further away.

Be the driver in your life. Don't let circumstances and other people's plans relegate you to the passenger seat. Ask yourself daily: *Does this lead me closer to my dream or further away from it?* That's your compass.

Today is a very important day! It's the beginning of a brand new chapter—as long as you choose it.

XOXO
The Universe

110

What Do You Have to Let Go of?

Sometimes, opening up to and attracting love is all about letting go. I know you've probably heard this a million times, but give me a minute to really explain, so you can put it into practice.

How many little daily problems and worries and hassles are you holding on to right now? How many responsibilities are you focused on at any given moment? How many little things are you upset over, irritated about, drained from, anchored down by? If you can let go of those ultimately insignificant things that are constantly pulling at you, you can open up to love and welcome it in. Properly. There won't be room for love otherwise, because you'll be so busy with your "stuff."

So, let go of the parking space you missed, or the cashier who gave you a snarky look at the checkout; let go of the guilt from your missed gym session or dentist appointment; let go of the mistake you made at work; let go of the ex you keep returning to in your mind to go over old arguments with; let go of the scratch in the side of your car; let go of your friend's insensitive comment when you shared your hopes and wishes; let go of the teacher who, 20 years ago, made you feel dumb; let go of all those little niggling things that will keep pulling at your attention and your energy if you let them.

Let go. Relax your shoulders, unclench your jaw. See the "issues" floating away. Now you're open. Now love has a home. If love had showed up when you had your attention on all those insignificant things, you wouldn't even have known it was there. *Now* you're ready for love.

XOXO
The Universe

111

Darkness Is Just the Seeming Absence of Light

*Y*ou may not have realized this, but the sun is always shining above the clouds, and throughout human existence, it always has been! It may seem hidden at times—yes, sometimes it may even seem as if all is dark… But know that this is always an illusion. The light is always shining. It never dims. It just gets temporarily obscured at times. Know this, and you will sense the light and the love no matter which clouds are traveling by. The light never stops shining.

And you know what? That light is inside you too. This is the message I want you to take from this whole book: That light is always there and there is always a way—to love, to your happiness. Know that you don't need to find the light on the outside. The light shines inside you and it did all along. Invite it to show itself to you, and it will.

You are never alone. Consciousness knows no bounds. Energy never dies. I am always with you and all around you. I am you, and I am everyone who existed before you. You are the one writing this, and I am the one reading. We are one and the same.

When you return to me, we will have a good laugh about this. Until then, I'll keep trying to show you. That all is well; that you are a soul made from light; that darkness is just the seeming absence of light—and that darkness is when people have forgotten that they are the light.

Remember this: You are never truly lost. You are never truly alone. The light never truly stops shining.

All My Love
The Universe

Afterword

*N*othing happens by accident. Someone, somewhere out there knew you would be picking up this book. These messages were meant for you. Wherever you're at on your journey right now, I know there is love for you.

In all my work with clients, I've experienced that wonderful shifts can happen in such a short space of time once you start working on your energy and your core beliefs. You are here for a reason, and I believe in you!

I'm so glad you decided to pick up this book—I hope that it will keep providing you with comfort, insights, and understanding along your life's path, just as these messages did for me.

Moving Forward

To help you take the journey even further, I've created a Free Love Transformation Pack for you, which you can access via my website: www.CassadyCayne.com. This includes a 45-minute Heart Activation Coaching and Energy Clearing Session and an e-book of distilled insights from my work with clients: *11 Keys To Attracting And Keeping True Love & 11 Blocks That Keep People From Their Ideal Relationship*.

These free gifts have been specially created to help you cleanse out old energies of hurt and disappointment, activate your heart to attract love, and assist you in uplifting and experiencing more joy in your life. You can also learn more about my work with transformational love coaching and energy healing on my website.

I would also love to hear from you about your experiences with this book! And I'd be thrilled if you wanted to recommend it or lend it to friends, family, or colleagues who might benefit from these messages; or write a review where you got the book so others can know what it's all about.

Let's spread the uplifting power of love far and wide!

You can find me at:

f **@cassadycayne** and **@twinflames1111**

⊙ **@cassady.cayne** and **@twin_flames_1111**

Cassady x

ABOUT THE AUTHOR

Cassady Cayne is a spiritual author and lightworker, founder of Twin Flames 11:11, and creator of The Love Blueprint transformational energy healing method.

After a sudden spiritual awakening five years ago, Cassady started a blog to share high-vibrational channeled messages and resources with others in ascension—working to help people connect with their inner divinity and their soul's purpose. She loves connecting with readers via social media and currently has close to 500,000 followers across various channels.

As a love and relationships coach and energy healer, Cassady's work focuses on getting people in touch with their intuition, unlocking their inner light, and empowering them on their journey to believing in themselves and living their highest path.

Originally from Scandinavia, Cassady now lives in Los Angeles, California, and enjoys learning, growing, and reaching ever further into her potential—sharing love and light with an ever-expanding community of seekers.

www.cassadycayne.com

HAY HOUSE

Look within

Join the conversation about latest products,
events, exclusive offers and more.

f Hay House

𝕏 @HayHouseUK

◉ @hayhouseuk

♥ healyourlife.com

We'd love to hear from you!